TEACHER'S PET PUBLICATIONS

LITPLAN TEACHER PACK
for
Esperanza Rising
based on the novel by
Pam Munoz Ryan

Written by
Maggie Magno

© 2008 Teacher's Pet Publications
All Rights Reserved

Copyright Teacher's Pet Publications 2008

Only the student materials in this unit plan (such as worksheets, study questions, and tests) may be reproduced multiple times for use in the purchaser's classroom.

For any additional copyright questions, contact Teacher's Pet Publications.

www.tpet.com

TABLE OF CONTENTS - *Esperanza Rising*

Introduction	5
Unit Objectives	7
Reading Assignment Sheet	8
Unit Outline	9
Study Questions (Short Answer)	13
Quiz/Study Questions (Multiple Choice)	22
Pre-reading Vocabulary Worksheets	45
Lesson One (Introductory Lesson)	69
Non-fiction Assignment Sheet	78
Oral Reading Evaluation Form	73
Writing Assignment 1	83
Writing Assignment 2	88
Writing Assignment 3	92
Project	71
Writing Evaluation Form	84
Vocabulary Review Activities	93
Extra Writing Assignments/Discussion ?s	95
Unit Review Activities	101
Unit Tests	107
Unit Resource Materials	165
Vocabulary Resource Materials	183

ABOUT THE AUTHOR

Pam Munoz Ryan

Pam Munoz Ryan grew up in California's San Joaquin Valley. She is the oldest of three sisters. She grew up with many of her aunts, uncles, cousins, and grandparents nearby. She is Spanish, Mexican, Basque, Italian, and Oklahoman. She received her Bachelor's and Master's Degrees at San Diego State University. She now lives in north San Diego County with her husband and four children.

She based *Esperanza Rising* on the experiences of her maternal grandmother who immigrated to the United States and worked in a farm labor camp. Relatives on both sides of her family, from both Mexico and Oklahoma, also worked in the fields.

Sources:
 http://www.pammunozryan.com/bio.htm
 Ryan, Pam Munoz. *Esperanza Rising*. New York: Scholastic, 2000.

Major Works
Riding Freedom
Amelia and Eleanor Go for a Ride
When Marian Sang
Mice and Beans
Becoming Naomi Leon
Paint the Wind
Esperanza Rising

Awards
Esperanza Rising:
 Pura Belpre Medal
 Jane Addams Peace Award
 ALA Top Ten Best Book for Young Adults
 Americas Award Honors Book

Riding Freedom:
 Willa Cather Award
 California Young Reader Medal

When Marian Sang:
 ALA Sibert Honor
 NCTE's Orbis Pictus Award

INTRODUCTION *Esperanza Rising*

This LitPlan has been designed to develop students' reading, writing, thinking, and language skills through exercises and activities related to *Esperanza Rising*. It includes eighteen lessons, supported by extra resource materials.

The **introductory lesson** introduces students to proverbs and the main themes of the novel. Following the introductory activity, students are given a transition to explain how the activity relates to the book they are about to read. Following the transition, students are given the materials they will be using during the unit. At the end of the lesson, students will be given the instructions for their journal projects.

The **reading assignments** are approximately thirty pages each; some are a little shorter while others are a little longer. Students have approximately 15 minutes of pre-reading work to do prior to each assignment. This pre-reading work involves reviewing the study questions for the assignment and doing some vocabulary work for selected vocabulary words they will encounter in their reading.

The **study guide questions** are fact-based questions; students can find the answers to these questions right in the text. These questions come in two formats: short answer or multiple choice. The best use of these materials is probably to use the short answer version of the questions as study guides for students (since answers will be more complete), and to use the multiple choice version for occasional quizzes.

The **vocabulary work** is intended to enrich students' vocabularies as well as to aid in the students' understanding of the book. Prior to each reading assignment, students will complete a two-part worksheet for selected vocabulary words in the upcoming reading assignment. Part I focuses on students' use of the general knowledge and contextual clues by giving the sentence in which the word appears in the text. Students are then to write down what they think the words mean based on the words' usage. Part II nails down the definitions of the words by giving students dictionary definitions of the words and having students match the words to the correct definitions based on the words' contextual usage. Students should then have an understanding of the words when they meet them in the text.

After each reading assignment, students will go back and formulate answers for the study guide questions. Discussion of these questions serves as a **review** of the most important events and ideas presented in the reading assignments.

After students complete reading the work, there is a **vocabulary review** lesson which pulls together all of the fragmented vocabulary lists for the reading assignments and gives students a review of all the words they have studied.

Following the vocabulary review, a lesson is devoted to the **extra discussion questions/writing assignments**. These questions focus on interpretation, critical analysis, and personal response employing a variety of thinking skills and adding to the students' understanding of the novel.

There is an **individual theme project** in this unit. Students will rewrite the story through the eyes of one of the characters.

There are three **writing assignments** in this unit, each with the purpose of informing, persuading, or expressing personal opinions. In Writing Assignment 1, students write a personal narrative in which they tell about a time when they had a sudden change of environment, like Esperanza. In Writing Assignment 2, students will write a persuasive essay in which they argue for or against striking for better working conditions. In Writing Assignment 3, students will respond to the literature by describing what they have learned from the story.

There is a **non-fiction reading assignment**. Students must read non-fiction articles, books, etc. to gather information about their themes in our world today.

The **review lesson** pulls together all the aspects of the unit. The teacher is given several choices of activities or games to use which all serve the same basic function of reviewing all of the information presented in the unit.

The **unit test** comes in two formats: multiple choice or short answer. As a convenience, two different tests for each format have been included. There is also an advanced short answer unit test for advanced students.

There are additional **support materials** included with this unit. The **Unit Resource Materials** section includes suggestions for an in-class library, crossword and word search puzzles related to the novel, and extra worksheets. There is a list of **bulletin board ideas** which gives the teacher suggestions for bulletin boards to go along with this unit. In addition, there is a list of **extra class activities** the teacher could choose from to enhance the unit or as a substitution for an exercise the teacher might feel is inappropriate for his/her class. **Answer keys** are located directly after the **reproducible student materials** throughout the unit. The **Vocabulary Resource Materials** section includes similar worksheets and games to reinforce the vocabulary words.

The **level** of this unit can be varied depending upon the criteria on which the individual assignments are graded, the teacher's expectations of his/her students in class discussions, and the formats chosen for the study guides, quizzes, and test. If teachers have other ideas/activities they wish to use, they can often be easily inserted prior to the review lesson.

The student materials may be reproduced for use in the teacher's classroom without infringement of copyrights. No other portion of this unit may be reproduced without the written consent of Teacher's Pet Publications, Inc.

UNIT OBJECTIVES *Esperanza Rising*

1. Students will define and discuss metaphors, symbols, and the themes in *Esperanza Rising*.

2. Students will practice reading orally and silently.

3. Students will answer questions to demonstrate their knowledge and understanding of the main events and characters in *Esperanza Rising*.

4. Students will study vocabulary from the book to better understand the book and to enrich their own vocabularies.

5. Students will read aloud, report, and participate in large and small group discussions to improve their public speaking and personal interaction skills.

6. Students will retell the story through the eyes of one of the characters.

7. Students will read non-fiction text that relates to *Esperanza Rising*.

8. Students will think logically and critically.

9. Students will demonstrate the ability to write effectively to inform by developing and organizing facts to convey information. Students will demonstrate the ability to write effectively to persuade by selecting and organizing relevant information, establishing an argumentative purpose, and by designing an appropriate strategy for an identified audience. Students will demonstrate the ability to write effectively to express personal ideas by selecting a form and its appropriate elements.

READING ASSIGNMENTS *Esperanza Rising*

Date Assigned	Assignment	Completion Date
	Assignment 1 Aguascalientes, Mexico & Las Uvas 1	
	Assignment 2 Las Papayas & Los Higos	
	Assignment 3 Las Guayabas	
	Assignment 4 Los Melones	
	Assignment 5 Las Cebollas	
	Assignment 6 Las Almendras & Las Ciruelas	
	Assignment 7 Las Papas	
	Assignment 8 Los Aguacates	
	Assignment 9 Los Esparragos & Los Duraznos	
	Assignment 10 Las Uvas 2	

UNIT OUTLINE *Esperanza Rising*

1	2	3	4	5
Introduction Journal Project	PVR 1 Foreshadowing Metaphors	Study ?s 1 PVR 2 Fruit/Vegetables Worksheet	Study ?s 2 PVR 3 Non-fiction Reading Assignment	Study ?s 3 PVR 4
6	7	8	9	10
Study ?s 4 PVR 5 Conflict	Study ?s 5 PVR 6 Writing Assignment #1	Study ?s 6 PVR 7	Study ?s 7 PVR 8 Writing Conferences	Study ?s 8 PVR 9 Writing Assignment #2
11	12	13	14	15
Study ?s 9 PVR 10	Study ?s 10 Writing Assignment #3 Writing Conferences	Vocabulary Review	Extra Discussion Questions	Extra Discussion Questions Continued
16	17	18		
Non-fiction Reports	Unit Review	Unit Test		

Key: P = Preview Study Questions   V = Vocabulary Work   R = Read

STUDY GUIDE QUESTIONS

STUDY GUIDE QUESTIONS *Esperanza Rising*

Assignment 1
<u>Aguascalientes, Mexico & Las Uvas 1</u>
1. Why do Papa and Esperanza lie flat on the ground?
2. What job does Esperanza do that is typically reserved for the eldest son of a wealthy rancher?
3. What event is Esperanza looking forward to that takes place three weeks after the harvest?
4. What thought comes to Esperanza after she pricks her finger on the thorn?
5. Abuelita is described as a smaller, older, more wrinkled version of Esperanza's mama. What makes her different than Mama and sometimes surprising?
6. Who is Hortensia? According to Esperanza, how does she compare to Mama?
7. Who are Alfonso and Miguel?
8. Who are Tio Luis and Tio Marco? What do they bring to Mama the night Papa is late coming home?
9. Miguel and Alfonso return to the ranch after searching for Papa. Why does Mama faint?

Assignment 2
<u>Las Papayas & Los Higos</u>
1. How does Papa die?
2. What does Senor Rodriguez bring to the ranch the day after Papa dies?
3. What is Tio Luis wearing that makes Esperanza shed angry tears?
4. Why doesn't Mama inherit Papa's land upon his death?
5. Why does Tio Luis want to marry Mama?
6. What is the one item that Esperanza manages to save from being burned in the house fire?
7. Who rescues Abuelita from the house fire?
8. Who is responsible for setting fire to El Rancho de las Rosas?
9. To whom are Esperanza and Mama indebted for their finances and their future?
10. Who helps Mama and Esperanza obtain traveling papers and clothes?

Assignment 3
<u>Las Guayabas</u>
1. Why doesn't Marisol come with Senor Rodriguez to say goodbye to Esperanza on the night she flees Aguascalientes?
2. Why do Mama, Esperanza, and Hortensia have to ride in the hidden compartment of the wagon?
3. How did Papa reward Miguel for protecting Esperanza when bandits rob the house?
4. How does Esperanza feel about riding in the train car from Zacatecas?
5. What is Miguel's dream job?
6. Why is Esperanza shocked that Mama is telling Carmen "the egg woman" about their troubles?

Assignment 4
Los Melones
1. Who meets Esperanza and the other travelers at the train station in California?
2. What does Esperanza think the first time she sees Isabel?
3. Why does Esperanza become upset when the family stops for lunch on their way to the camp?
4. What is Isabel most looking forward to now that she lives at the new camp in Arvin?
5. Who is Marta?
6. According to Marta, why don't the field owners mix workers of different ethnic groups?

Assignment 5
Las Cebollas
1. Of what does Esperanza's new home, the camp cabin, remind her?
2. Why do Esperanza and Mama have to share a cabin with Hortensia and Alfonso?
3. What are Esperanza's two jobs at the camp?
4. About what does Isabel continually ask Esperanza to tell her?
5. What is Mama's job at the camp?
6. What does Miguel teach Esperanza to do after she is ridiculed by Marta and her friends?

Assignment 6
Las Almendras & Las Ciruelas
1. With what do Miguel and Alfonso surprise Mama and Esperanza?
2. Why doesn't Esperanza want to go to the jamaica?
3. What does Marta announce at the jamaica?
4. Esperanza tells Mama that she will pray for many things in church, but what does she pray for most of all?
5. What does Mama say she will pray for?
6. What does Esperanza feed Lupe and Pepe that makes them sick?
7. To Isabel's surprise, what does Esperanza do to help the twins feel better?
8. How does the dust storm affect Mama?

Assignment 7
Las Papas
1. What item does Mama ask for that Esperanza takes out of her valise?
2. Why does the doctor recommend that Mama to go to the hospital?
3. Why does Esperanza start working?
4. What is Esperanza's first job?
5. Marta's aunt shares some news that causes the working women to worry. What is the news?
6. How does Esperanza spend her Christmas?

Assignment 8
Los Aguacates
1. What does Esperanza do with the money she earns from her job?
2. Why does the doctor forbid Esperanza from seeing Mama in the hospital?
3. Why do Miguel and Esperanza shop at Mr. Yakota's market when there are other markets much closer to the camp?
4. What are the living conditions at the strikers' camp?
5. What does Esperanza give the campesino family who are just arriving at the strikers' camp?
6. What happens to Miguel that causes everyone in the cabin to celebrate?

Assignment 9
Los Esparragos & Los Duraznos
1. Why does a man with a gun ride on the truck with Esperanza and the other working women?
2. What do the strikers do to disrupt the work in the packing shed?
3. Why do the strikers drop their picket signs and scatter into the fields?
4. How does Esperanza help Marta?
5. Why is Isabel praying at the washtub grotto every night after dinner?
6. What luxuries will the new camp for the workers from Oklahoma have?
7. Why does Miguel lose his job as a mechanic at the railroad?
8. What special present does Esperanza give to Isabel? Why?

Assignment 10
Las Uvas 2
1. Who steals all of Esperanza's money orders?
2. Why does Alfonso come to get Esperanza at the shed?
3. Who gets off the bus with Miguel?
4. What does Esperanza finally finish making?
5. A few days before Esperanza's birthday, she begs Miguel to drive her to the foothills before sunrise. Why?
6. What is Esperanza's birthday surprise?

STUDY GUIDE QUESTIONS ANSWER KEY *Esperanza Rising*

Assignment 1
<u>Aguascalientes, Mexico & Las Uvas 1</u>

1. Why do Papa and Esperanza lie flat on the ground?
   Papa tells Esperanza that when one lies down on the land, one can feel it breathe and its heart beating. He is explaining to Esperanza that the whole valley breathes and lives. Esperanza wants to experience this, so Papa has her lie flat on the ground next to him with her cheek pressed against the earth.

2. What job does Esperanza do that is typically reserved for the eldest son of a wealthy rancher?
   Esperanza cuts the first bunch of grapes with a special knife signaling the beginning of the harvest season.

3. What event is Esperanza looking forward to that takes place three weeks after the harvest?
   She is looking forward to the fiesta that celebrates both the end of the harvest season and her birthday.

4. What thought comes to Esperanza after she pricks her finger on the thorn?
   She automatically thinks, "bad luck."

5. Abuelita is described as a smaller, older, more wrinkled version of Esperanza's mama. What makes her different than Mama and sometimes surprising?
   Although some things are always the same with Abuelita, others are surprising: a flower in her hair, a beautiful stone in her pocket, or a philosophical saying salted into her conversation, for example.

6. Who is Hortensia? According to Esperanza, how does she compare to Mama?
   Hortensia is the housekeeper. Esperanza thinks Hortensia is the opposite of Mama.

7. Who are Alfonso and Miguel?
   Alfonso is Hortensia's husband and el jefe, the boss of the field-workers. He is also Papa's close friend and companion. Miguel is Alfonso and Hortensia's son.

8. Who are Tio Luis and Tio Marco? What do they bring to Mama the night Papa is late coming home?
   They are Papa's older stepbrothers. Tio Luis is the bank president and Tio Marco is the mayor of the town. They bring Mama the silver belt buckle that belongs to Papa--a sign that something bad may have happened to him.

9. Miguel and Alfonso return to the ranch after searching for Papa. Why does Mama faint?
   They have Papa's body in the back of the wagon.

Assignment 2
<u>Las Papayas & Los Higos</u>

1. How does Papa die?
   Papa and his vaqueros are ambushed and killed by bandits while mending a fence on the farthest reaches of the ranch.

2. What does Senor Rodriguez bring to the ranch the day after Papa dies?
   Senor Rodriguez brings the papayas that Papa had ordered for the fiesta.

3. What is Tio Luis wearing that makes Esperanza shed angry tears?
   He is wearing Papa's silver belt buckle with the brand of the ranch on it.

4. Why doesn't Mama inherit Papa's land upon his death?
   It isn't customary to leave land to women.

5. Why does Tio Luis want to marry Mama?
   Tio Luis wants to enter politics, and he needs Mama's influence among the people to win an election. Mama is loved and respected by the people in the region.
6. What is the one item that Esperanza manages to save from being burned in the house fire?
   Esperanza saves the last doll her Papa gave her.
7. Who rescues Abuelita from the house fire?
   Miguel rescues Abuelita.
8. Who is responsible for setting fire to El Rancho de las Rosas?
   Tio Luis and Tio Marco are responsible for the fire.
9. To whom are Esperanza and Mama indebted for their finances and their future?
   Mama and Esperanza are indebted to Hortensia and Alfonso.
10. Who helps Mama and Esperanza obtain traveling papers and clothes?
    Abuelita's sisters help Mama and Esperanza. Because they are nuns, they are able to obtain the items very discreetly without Tio Luis finding out.

Assignment 3
Las Guayabas

1. Why doesn't Marisol come with Senor Rodriguez to say goodbye to Esperanza on the night she flees Aguascalientes?
   Marisol doesn't come to say goodbye because she doesn't know Esperanza is leaving. Senor Rodriguez cannot risk telling anyone about Esperanza and Mama's departure, not even his own daughter.
2. Why do Mama, Esperanza, and Hortensia have to ride in the hidden compartment of the wagon?
   They have to hide because it isn't safe for women to be out at night. There are too many bandits in the region. Also, Tio Luis might have spies who would be looking for anything suspicious happening on the ranch.
3. How did Papa reward Miguel for protecting Esperanza when bandits rob the house?
   Papa treated Miguel to a day-long train ride to Zacatecas.
4. How does Esperanza feel about riding in the train car from Zacatecas?
   She does not want to travel in the car because it is not clean and the people do not look trustworthy to her.
5. What is Miguel's dream job?
   He wants to work for the railroad.
6. Why is Esperanza shocked that Mama is telling Carmen "the egg woman" about their troubles?
   Esperanza is shocked because when they lived in Aguascalientes, Mama would have said it was inappropriate to tell an "egg woman" their problems. Mama explains to Esperanza that it is all right to tell their problems to peasants because they are now peasants too.

Assignment 4
Los Melones

1. Who meets Esperanza and the other travelers at the train station in California?
   Alfonso's brother, Juan, and his family meet the travelers at the station to take them to the camp.
2. What does Esperanza think the first time she sees Isabel?
   She cannot help but think how much Isabel looks like the doll her father had given her.
3. Why does Esperanza become upset when the family stops for lunch on their way to the camp?
   Esperanza becomes upset because she can't hear the heartbeat of the valley like she could at El Rancho de las Rosas.
4. What is Isabel most looking forward to now that she lives at the new camp in Arvin?
   She is looking forward to going to school for the first time.
5. Who is Marta?
   Marta is a girl about Miguel's age who lives in a camp where they pick cotton.
6. According to Marta, why don't the field owners mix workers of different ethnic groups?
   Marta claims the owners don't want the workers banding together for higher wages or better housing.

Assignment 5
Las Cebollas

1. Of what does Esperanza's new home, the camp cabin, remind her?
   It reminds her of the horse stables at El Rancho de las Rosas.
2. Why do Esperanza and Mama have to share a cabin with Hortensia and Alfonso?
   They have to share a cabin because at this family camp there is no housing for single women. The landowner will only give one cabin for each man and his family.
3. What are Esperanza's two jobs at the camp?
   She is responsible for taking care of the twins and sweeping the platform.
4. About what does Isabel continually ask Esperanza to tell her?
   Isabel wants to know about Esperanza's life when she was rich.
5. What is Mama's job at the camp?
   Mama works in the shed packing grapes.
6. What does Miguel teach Esperanza to do after she is ridiculed by Marta and her friends?
   Miguel teaches Esperanza how to sweep.

Assignment 6
Las Almendras & Las Ciruelas

1. With what do Miguel and Alfonso surprise Mama and Esperanza?
   They have brought roses from Papa's garden and have planted them behind the camp cabin.
2. Why doesn't Esperanza want to go to the jamaica?
   She is embarrassed because the whole camp knows she doesn't know how to sweep. She also doesn't want to see Marta who ridiculed her for not knowing how to sweep.
3. What does Marta announce at the jamaica?
   She announces that the cotton workers will strike the following day, and she asks for everyone to join the strike to make a more powerful statement.

4. Esperanza tells Mama that she will pray for many things in church, but what does she pray for most of all?
   She will pray that Abuelita will get well, that she will be able to get her money from Tio Luis's bank, and that she will soon join Mama and Esperanza in California.
5. What does Mama say she will pray for?
   She will pray for the same things as Esperanza and that Esperanza will be strong, no matter what happens.
6. What does Esperanza feed Lupe and Pepe that makes them sick?
   She feeds them plums.
7. To Isabel's surprise, what does Esperanza do to help the twins feel better?
   She feeds them rice water.
8. How does the dust storm affect Mama?
   Because of the storm, Mama gets Valley Fever.

Assignment 7
Las Papas

1. What item does Mama ask for that Esperanza takes out of her valise?
   Mama asks for Abuelita's unfinished blanket.
2. Why does the doctor recommend that Mama to go to the hospital?
   The doctor says Mama is not getting any better, and she is depressed. He thinks she needs nursing around the clock in order to get well.
3. Why does Esperanza start working?
   Esperanza starts working because she wants to help Abuelita come to California. She believes Mama needs Abuelita in order to get well.
4. What is Esperanza's first job?
   Her first job is cutting potato eyes.
5. Marta's aunt shares some news that causes the working women to worry. What is the news?
   She tells the women that the Mexicans who do not strike might be in danger. They may be harmed by those who do strike.
6. How does Esperanza spend her Christmas?
   She spends her Christmas with Mama at the hospital. She crochets and talks to Mama, but Mama sleeps the whole time Esperanza is there.

Assignment 8
Los Aguacates

1. What does Esperanza do with the money she earns from her job?
   Esperanza buys a money order at the market and stores it in her valise.
2. Why does the doctor forbid Esperanza from seeing Mama in the hospital?
   Esperanza is not allowed to see her because Mama has developed pneumonia. The doctor doesn't want visitors to bring in any new germs because Mama's immune system is weak.
3. Why do Miguel and Esperanza shop at Mr. Yakota's market when there are other markets much closer to the camp?
   They shop at Mr. Yakota's market because he is kind to Mexicans, and he stocks many of the foods that Mexicans like. Many of the other markets do not treat the Mexicans kindly.

4. What are the living conditions at the strikers' camp?
   There are ten toilets for hundreds of people. Some people live in tents but others only have burlap bags stretched between poles. The kitchens are outdoors. In an irrigation ditch, women are washing clothes and children are bathing at the same time. Clotheslines run everywhere.
5. What does Esperanza give the campesino family who are just arriving at the strikers' camp?
   She gives them a hatful of beans and the pinata full of caramels that she had purchased for Mama.
6. What happens to Miguel that causes everyone in the cabin to celebrate?
   Miguel gets a new job working for the railroad.

Assignment 9
Los Esparragos & Los Duraznos

1. Why does a man with a gun ride on the truck with Esperanza and the other working women?
   The man with the gun is on the truck to protect the workers from the strikers.
2. What do the strikers do to disrupt the work in the packing shed?
   They hide razor blades, a rat, a rattle snake, and shards of glass in the asparagus boxes to slow the workers down.
3. Why do the strikers drop their picket signs and scatter into the fields?
   They scatter into the fields to hide from the immigration officials who have arrived to deport the strikers to Mexico.
4. How does Esperanza help Marta?
   Esperanza helps Marta avoid being captured by immigration. She gives her an apron so Marta looks like one of the workers instead of a striker.
5. Why is Isabel praying at the washtub grotto every night after dinner?
   Isabel is praying to become the Queen of May at her school. She wants to be "la reina" like Esperanza.
6. What luxuries will the new camp for the workers from Oklahoma have?
   The new camp will have toilets and hot water inside the cabins and a swimming pool.
7. Why does Miguel lose his job as a mechanic at the railroad?
   Miguel loses his job because a group of men from Oklahoma show up and offer to work for half the money.
8. What special present does Esperanza give to Isabel? Why?
   Esperanza gives Isabel her porcelain doll because Isabel was not chosen as the Queen of May.

Assignment 10
Las Uvas 2

1. Who steals all of Esperanza's money orders?
   Miguel steals Esperanza's money orders.
2. Why does Alfonso come to get Esperanza at the shed?
   Alfonso has received a message from Miguel asking him to bring Esperanza to the bus station at three o'clock.
3. Who gets off the bus with Miguel?
   Abuelita gets off the bus with Miguel; he has brought her back from Mexico.

4. What does Esperanza finally finish making?
   She finally finishes crocheting Abuelita's blanket.

5. A few days before Esperanza's birthday, she begs Miguel to drive her to the foothills before sunrise. Why?
   She wants to lie on the ground and feel it breathing and its heart beating. She asks Miguel to join her.

6. What is Esperanza's birthday surprise?
   Miguel, Alfonso, and Juan serenade her with the birthday song.

MULTIPLE CHOICE STUDY/QUIZ QUESTIONS
Esperanza Rising

Assignment 1
Aguascalientes, Mexico & Las Uvas 1

1. Why do Papa and Esperanza lie flat on the ground?
    A. They are attempting to hide from bandits who are angry with Papa.
    B. Esperanza has fallen while cutting the first fruit of the harvest season. Papa bends down to pick her up.
    C. Papa tells Esperanza that the whole valley breathes and lives. She wants to feel the land breathing and hear its heartbeat.
    D. They are playing a game of hide-and-go-seek.

2. What job does Esperanza do that is typically reserved for the eldest son of a wealthy farmer?
    A. She sharpens the blade used for cutting the first fruit of the harvest season.
    B. She helps Papa fix the machinery.
    C. She does chores on the ranch like cleaning the stables and mending fences.
    D. She cuts the first bunch of grapes with a special knife signaling the beginning of the harvest season.

3. What event is Esperanza looking forward to that takes place three weeks after the harvest?
    A. She is looking forward to her Quinceanera.
    B. She is looking forward to Abuelita teaching her how to crochet.
    C. She is looking forward to the fiesta that celebrates both the end of the harvest season and her birthday.
    D. She is looking forward to a play-date with her best friend Marisol Rodriguez.

4. What event occurs that causes Esperanza to think the words, "bad luck"?
    A. She finds her father's silver belt-buckle in the vineyard.
    B. She pricks herself with a thorn from a rose while waiting for Papa in the garden.
    C. She has a bad dream about her father.
    D. Her uncles Luis and Marco arrive for a visit.

5. Which statement best describes Abuelita?
   A. Abuelita is Papa's mother. She is a stern woman of whom Esperanza is frightened. She runs the household and bosses everyone around.
   B. Abuelita is a smaller, older, more wrinkled version of Mama. She looks very distinguished, wearing a respectable black dress, the same gold loops she wears in her ears every day, and her white hair pulled back into a bun at the nape of her neck.
   C. Abuelita is the housekeeper. She is an Indian from Oaxaco, with a short, solid figure and a braid down her back.
   D. Abuelita is a taller, younger version of Mama. She is Mama's younger sister and she wears bright colored clothing and fancy diamond jewelry every day.

6. Who is Hortensia?
   A. She is Esperanza's grandmother.
   B. She is the housekeeper.
   C. She is Mama's best friend.
   D. She is Esperanza's best-friend.

7. Who are Alfonso and Miguel?
   A. Alfonso is Hortensia's husband and Miguel is their son.
   B. Alfonso and Miguel are Esperanza's uncles who visit the ranch when Papa goes missing.
   C. Alfonso is Esperanza's uncle and Miguel is her cousin.
   D. Alfonso is a field-worker and Miguel is his best friend.

8. Who are Tio Luis and Tio Marco? What do they bring to Mama the night Papa is late coming home?
   A. They are campesinos who are unhappy working on the ranch. They bring Mama the silver belt buckle that belongs to Papa.
   B. They are Papa's best friends. They bring Mama gifts from the United States.
   C. They are Papa's older stepbrothers. Tio Luis is the bank president and Tio Marco is the mayor of the town. They bring Mama the silver belt buckle that belongs to Papa.
   D. They are Esperanza's favorite uncles. They bring Mama some chocolates and flowers.

9. Miguel and Alfonso return to the ranch after searching for Papa. Why does Mama faint?
    A. Papa is with them and she is so relieved to see he is home unharmed.
    B. She is afraid of Alfonso and Miguel.
    C. She sees a ghost.
    D. They have Papa's body in the back of the wagon.

Assignment 2
Las Papayas & Los Higos

1. How does Papa die?
    A. He falls off his horse and is trampled to death.
    B. He is killed by a wild animal while fixing the fence on the ranch.
    C. Tio Luis and Tio Marco murder him in his sleep.
    D. Papa and his vaqueros are ambushed and killed by bandits while mending a fence on the farthest reaches of the ranch.

2. What does Senor Rodriguez bring to the ranch the day after Papa dies?
    A. He brings Esperanza a doll - a present for her thirteenth birthday.
    B. He brings a rosary for Esperanza so she can pray for her father.
    C. He brings the papayas that Papa had ordered for the fiesta.
    D. He brings his daughter Marisol to comfort Esperanza.

3. What is Tio Luis wearing that makes Esperanza shed angry tears?
    A. He is wearing Papa's wedding ring.
    B. He's wearing Papa's hat - the one Esperanza gave him for his birthday.
    C. He is wearing Papa's silver belt buckle with the brand of the ranch on it.
    D. He isn't wearing black. He should be wearing black to honor his dead brother.

4. Why doesn't Mama inherit Papa's land upon his death?
    A. Mama is supposed to inherit the land, but Tio Luis and Tio Marco change Papa's will after he dies.
    B. It isn't customary to leave land to women.
    C. The land didn't belong to Papa. Tio Luis really owns the land.
    D. Mama doesn't want to live on the land anymore. It reminds her too much of Papa.

5. Why does Tio Luis want to marry Mama?
    A. Tio Luis wants to enter politics, and he needs Mama's influence among the people to win an election. Mama is loved and respected by the people of the region.
    B. Tio Luis loves Mama's house and wants to live in it. He has to marry her to do so.
    C. He wants to marry Mama so that Esperanza has a father figure in her life.
    D. He is in love with Mama and wants to take care of her in her time of need.

6. What is the one item that Esperanza manages to save from being burned in the house fire?
    A. She saves the rose Papa planted for her in his garden.
    B. She saves the last doll Papa gave her.
    C. She saves her trunk full of the items "for someday."
    D. She saves the shawl that Abuelita is crocheting.

7. Who rescues Abuelita from the house fire?
    A. Tio Luis
    B. Esperanza
    C. Alfonso
    D. Miguel

8. Who is responsible for setting fire to El Rancho de las Rosas?
    A. Campesinos
    B. Tio Luis and Tio Marco
    C. Bandits
    D. Miguel

9. To whom are Esperanza and Mama indebted for their finances and their future?
    A. Abuelita
    B. Tio Luis and Tio Marco
    C. Hortensia and Alfonso
    D. Senor Rodriguez

10. Who helps Mama and Esperanza obtain traveling papers and clothes?
    A. Tio Luis and Tio Marco
    B. Hortensia and Alfonso
    C. Senor Rodriguez
    D. Abuelita's sisters

Assignment 3
Las Guayabas

1. Why doesn't Marisol come with Senor Rodriguez to say goodbye to Esperanza on the night she flees Aguascalientes?
    A. Marisol doesn't know Esperanza is leaving because Senor Rodriguez cannot risk telling anyone about Esperanza and Mama's departure.
    B. Marisol wants to say goodbye but her father won't let her because it is too dangerous.
    C. Marisol is too busy playing with her other friends.
    D. Marisol is angry with Esperanza for leaving.

2. Why do Mama, Esperanza, and Hortensia have to ride in the hidden compartment of the wagon?
    A. They have a long way to travel and the compartment allows them to lay down and sleep.
    B. Women are not allowed to travel at night.
    C. Women are not allowed to travel with men who are not related to them.
    D. They have to hide because it isn't safe for women to be out at night. There are bandits and Tio Luis might have spies watching the ranch.

3. How did Papa reward Miguel for protecting Esperanza when bandits were robbing the house?
    A. Papa told Miguel he could one day marry Esperanza.
    B. Papa gave Miguel a new suit.
    C. Papa gave Miguel money.
    D. Papa treated Miguel to a day-long train ride to Zacatecas.

4. Which statement best describes the train car in which Esperanza and Mama travel?
    A. The car is lined with tables covered in white linens and finely dressed servers are waiting to take lunch orders.
    B. The car is crowded with peasants sitting on wooden benches and trash is scattered on the floor.
    C. The car is clean and spacious with plenty of room for the well-dressed travelers to sit comfortably.
    D. The car is crowded with animals and hay is scattered all over the floor.

5. How does Esperanza feel about riding in the train car from Zacatecas?
   A. She is irritated because she has to share a seat with Miguel and she doesn't think it is appropriate for a young lady to sit next to a peasant.
   B. She does not want to travel in the car because it is not clean and the people do not look trustworthy to her.
   C. She is excited because the car is so luxurious.
   D. She is angry because the servers do not bring lunch quickly enough.

6. What is Miguel's dream job?
   A. He wants to work for the railroad.
   B. He wants to be the boss of the field-workers like his father.
   C. He wants to be in politics like Tio Marco.
   D. He wants to own a ranch like Papa some day.

7. Why is Esperanza shocked that Mama is telling Carmen "the egg woman" about their troubles?
   A. Esperanza is shocked because when they lived in Aguascalientes Mama would have said it was inappropriate to tell "an egg woman" their problems.
   B. Esperanza thinks Mama should not talk to strangers, especially since Tio Luis could have spies on the lookout.
   C. Esperanza thinks the "egg woman" is ugly and Mama should only talk to beautiful women.
   D. Esperanza thinks Mama is being mean to the woman and she's ashamed of Mama's behavior.

Assignment 4
Los Melones

1. Who meets Esperanza and the other travelers at the train station in California?
    A. Abuelita
    B. Tio Luis and Tio Marco
    C. Immigration Officials
    D. Juan, Josefina, Isabel, and the Twins

2. What does Esperanza think the first time she sees Isabel?
    A. She thinks Isabel looks like the doll her father gave her.
    B. She thinks Isabel is a very interesting character, and she wants to have a chance to talk with her about her travels.
    C. She thinks Isabel is a whining crybaby.
    D. She thinks she and Isabel will become best friends.

3. Why does Esperanza become upset when the family stops for lunch on their way to the camp?
    A. She misses her father.
    B. Mama becomes angry with Esperanza because of her bad attitude.
    C. Esperanza becomes upset because she can't hear the heartbeat of the valley.
    D. Esperanza and Miguel get into an argument.

4. What is Isabel most looking forward to now that she lives at the new camp in Arvin?
    A. She is looking forward to going to school for the first time.
    B. She is looking forward to being able to work in the sheds with her mother.
    C. She is looking forward to having a toilet in the cabin.
    D. She is looking forward to making new friends.

5. Who is Marta?
    A. Marta is a girl about Miguel's age who lives in a camp where they pick cotton.
    B. Marta is the name of the doll Esperanza got from her father.
    C. Marta is a young girl Esperanza meets on the train.
    D. Marta is Esperanza's grandmother.

6. According to Marta, why don't the field owners mix workers of different ethnic groups?
    A. Marta doesn't know why the owners keep the workers from mixing.
    B. Marta claims that the owners don't want the workers banding together for higher wages or better housing.
    C. Marta claims the owners think the workers are more efficient when they are with other people from the same culture who speak the same language.
    D. Marta claims the owners are racist and don't want the Mexicans mixing with any other races.

Assignment 5
Las Cebollas

1. Of what does Esperanza's new home, the camp cabin, remind her?
    A. It reminds her of her beautiful house at El Rancho de las Rosas.
    B. It reminds her of Marisol's house.
    C. It reminds her of the servants' cabins at El Rancho de las Rosas.
    D. It reminds her of the horse stables at El Rancho de las Rosas.

2. Why do Esperanza and Mama have to share a cabin with Hortensia and Alfonso?
    A. The landowner will only give one cabin for each man and his family; there is no housing for single women.
    B. Hortensia and Alfonso need Esperanza to clean the cabin and cook while they are at work.
    C. Mama doesn't want to be separated from her only friends in the United States.
    D. Mama and Esperanza can't afford the rent for their own cabin.

3. What are Esperanza's two jobs at the camp?
    A. She is responsible for cleaning the toilets and peeling onions.
    B. She is responsible for crocheting and mending clothes.
    C. She is responsible for taking care of the twins and sweeping the platform.
    D. She is responsible for picking onions and washing dishes.

4. About what does Isabel continually ask Esperanza to tell her?
    A. Isabel wants Esperanza to teach her Spanish.
    B. Isabel wants to hear stories about Esperanza's father.
    C. Isabel has a crush on Miguel and wants Esperanza to tell her all about him.
    D. Isabel wants to know about Esperanza's life when she was rich.

5. What is Mama's job at the camp?
    A. Mama picks grapes in the fields.
    B. Mama is responsible for sweeping the platform.
    C. Mama is responsible for watching the twins while Josefina is at work.
    D. Mama works in the shed packing grapes.

6. What does Miguel teach Esperanza to do after she is ridiculed by Marta and her friends?
    A. Miguel teaches Esperanza how to sweep.
    B. Miguel teaches Esperanza how to fix a motor.
    C. Miguel teaches Esperanza how to speak English.
    D. Miguel teaches Esperanza how to wash clothes.

Assignment 6
Las Almendras & Las Ciruelas

1. With what do Miguel and Alfonso surprise Mama and Esperanza?
    A. They have Josefina make a flan especially for Mama and Esperanza.
    B. They have bought a pinata full of caramels for Mama and Esperanza.
    C. They have brought roses from Papa's garden and have planted them behind the camp cabin.
    D. They give Mama and Esperanza a picture of Papa that they rescued from the fire.

2. Why doesn't Esperanza want to go to the jamaica?
    A. She doesn't like to dance.
    B. She doesn't know anyone and is afraid she will be lonely.
    C. She doesn't have a pretty dress to wear.
    D. She is embarrassed because the whole camp knows she doesn't know how to sweep.

3. What does Marta announce at the jamaica?
    A. She announces that the cotton workers will strike the following day.
    B. She announces that she is selling a box full of kittens.
    C. She announces that Esperanza doesn't know how to sweep.
    D. She announces her engagement to Miguel.

4. Esperanza tells Mama that she will pray for many things in church, but what does she pray for most of all?
    A. She prays for Mama to earn enough money so they can leave the camp.
    B. She prays that the days will get easier at the camp.
    C. She prays that Abuelita will get well and that she will soon join Mama and Esperanza in California.
    D. She prays that Marta will leave her alone.

5. What does Mama say she will pray for?
    A. She prays that Esperanza will be strong, no matter what happens.
    B. She prays that she will earn enough money to buy a home for herself and Esperanza.
    C. She prays that she will someday have dresses like she did in Mexico.
    D. She prays that she will find a husband that can take care of her and her daughter.

6. What does Esperanza feed Lupe and Pepe that makes them sick?
    A. Almonds
    B. Cantaloupes
    C. Onions
    D. Plums

7. To Isabel's surprise, what does Esperanza do to help the twins feel better?
    A. She puts cool washcloths on their foreheads.
    B. She changes their diapers.
    C. She feeds them rice water.
    D. She rubs their tummies.

8. How does the dust storm affect Mama?
    A. Mama loves the storm because it reminds her of Mexico.
    B. The dust from the storm blinds Mama.
    C. Because of the storm, Mama gets Valley Fever.
    D. Mama becomes depressed because the storm causes Esperanza to get sick.

Assignment 7
Las Papas

1. What item does Mama ask for that Esperanza takes out of her valise?
    A. Mama asks for Esperanza's doll.
    B. Mama asks for Papa's belt with the silver buckle.
    C. Mama asks for Abuelita's unfinished blanket.
    D. Mama asks for a shawl to cover her shoulders.

2. Why does the doctor recommend that Mama to go to the hospital?
    A. Mama's illness is contagious and the doctor is concerned that the others will catch it.
    B. Mama's illness is getting worse every day and the doctor doesn't think she will live much longer.
    C. Mama needs special medications that are only available at the hospital.
    D. The doctor says Mama is not getting any better and that she is depressed.

3. Why does Esperanza start working?
    A. Esperanza starts working because she needs to help Hortensia and Alfonso pay the rent.
    B. Esperanza starts working because she wants to earn money to bring Abuelita to California.
    C. Esperanza starts working because Marta makes fun of her.
    D. Esperanza starts working because she wants to buy a ticket to return to Mexico.

4. What is Esperanza's first job?
    A. Sorting peaches
    B. Tying grape vines
    C. Cutting potato eyes
    D. Packing asparagus

5. Marta's aunt shares some news that causes the working women to worry. What is the news?
    A. She tells the women that Marta has run away.
    B. She tells the women that immigration is coming to send back workers who don't have their papers in order.
    C. She tells the women that the Mexicans who do not strike might be in danger.
    D. She tells the women that workers from Oklahoma might steal their jobs.

6. How does Esperanza spend her Christmas?
    A. She spends her Christmas with Mama at the hospital.
    B. She spends her Christmas on a train to Mexico in hopes of bringing Abuelita to California.
    C. She spends her Christmas packing potatoes in the sheds.
    D. She spends her Christmas praying in church that Mama will get better.

Assignment 8
Los Aguacates

1. What does Esperanza do with the money she earns from her job?
   A. Esperanza buys a money order at the market and stores it in her valise.
   B. She helps Hortensia and Alfonso pay for rent.
   C. She buys Mama a present.
   D. She buys Isabel a doll.

2. Why does the doctor forbid Esperanza from seeing Mama in the hospital?
   A. Esperanza is not allowed to see her because Mama has developed pneumonia.
   B. Mama has requested not to have any visitors.
   C. The doctor thinks Esperanza is causing Mama's illness to get worse.
   D. The doctor is racist and doesn't want too many Mexicans in the hospital.

3. Why do Miguel and Esperanza shop at Mr. Yakota's market when there are other markets much closer to the camp?
   A. Mr. Yakota is a good friend of the family.
   B. Mr. Yakota has discounted prices.
   C. Mr. Yakota is kind to Mexicans and he stocks many of the foods that Mexicans like.
   D. The owners of the farm have a deal with Mr. Yakota and force the workers to shop from his store.

4. Which statement best describes the strikers' camp?
   A. The camp is brand new with running hot water, indoor toilets, and a pool.
   B. There are plenty of cabins for everyone and they have running water indoors.
   C. There are ten toilets for hundreds of people, people live in tents, the kitchens are outdoors, and children bathe in an irrigation ditch.
   D. The camp is a little nicer than Esperanza's camp, but the strikers are paid less money.

5. What does Esperanza give the campesino family who are just arriving at the strikers' camp?
   A. She gives them a sack full of old clothes and a few yarn dolls.
   B. She gives them a hatful of beans and a pinata full of caramels.
   C. She gives them her money order that she has just purchased form Mr. Yakota's.
   D. She gives them the groceries she purchased from Mr. Yakota's market.

6. What happens to Miguel that makes everyone in the cabin celebrate?
    A. Miguel gets a raise.
    B. Miguel gets a new job working for the railroad.
    C. Miguel gets engaged.
    D. Miguel finds a new job in Northern California.

Assignment 9
Los Esparragos & Los Duraznos

1. Why was a man with a gun riding on the truck with Esperanza and the other working women?
    A. He was on the truck to keep the women from escaping.
    B. He was on the truck to protect the workers from the strikers.
    C. He was on the truck to intimidate the women and scare them into working harder.
    D. He was on the truck to keep the women from striking.

2. What do the strikers do to disrupt the work in the packing shed?
    A. They hide fireworks in the harvest hoping to burn down the farm.
    B. The strikers hide inside the harvest to avoid being picked up by the immigration officials.
    C. They hide razor blades, a rat, a rattle snake, and shards of glass in the asparagus to slow the workers down.
    D. They hide money for the workers so they can escape back to Mexico.

3. Why do the strikers drop their picket signs and scatter into the fields?
    A. They scatter into the fields to hide from the immigration officials who have arrived to deport the strikers to Mexico.
    B. They scatter into the fields because the workers are chasing after them.
    C. They scatter into the fields to hide from the men armed with guns.
    D. They scatter into the fields to scare the workers.

4. How does Esperanza help Marta?
    A. Esperanza gives Marta money to help her mother.
    B. Esperanza gives Marta food and shelter when she is kicked out of her camp.
    C. Esperanza helps Marta get a job at the farm.
    D. Esperanza gives Marta an apron so she looks like one of the workers and won't be arrested by immigration.

5. Why is Isabel praying at the washtub grotto every night after dinner?
    A. Isabel is praying to become the Queen of May at her school.
    B. Isabel is praying for money so she can have a life like Esperanza's.
    C. Isabel is praying for Mama to get better.
    D. Isabel is praying for a doll.

6. What luxuries will the new camp for the workers from Oklahoma have?
   A. The new camp will have a school for the children of the workers.
   B. The new camp will have a playground for the children and a grocery store.
   C. The new camp will have indoor toilets, running hot water, and a swimming pool.
   D. The new camp will have brand new cabins with enough beds for everyone.

7. Why does Miguel lose his job as a mechanic at the railroad?
   A. Miguel quits his job because it doesn't pay well enough.
   B. Miguel loses his job because he is late for work one day and it makes his boss angry.
   C. Miguel loses his job because he confronts his boss and asks for more money.
   D. Miguel loses his job because a group of men from Oklahoma show up and offer to work for half the money.

8. What special present does Esperanza give to Isabel? Why?
   A. Esperanza gives Isabel her porcelain doll because Isabel was not chosen as the Queen of May.
   B. Esperanza gives Isabel her money orders because Isabel was not chosen as the Queen of May.
   C. Esperanza gives Isabel Abuelita's blanket because Isabel was not chosen as the Queen of May.
   D. Esperanza gives Isabel a yarn doll to give to her best friend Sylvia who has never had a doll.

Assignment 10
Las Uvas 2

1. Who steals all of Esperanza's money orders?
    A. Miguel
    B. Marta
    C. Isabel
    D. The campesino family

2. Why does Alfonso come to get Esperanza at the shed?
    A. Mama's illness has returned and she has sent Alfonso to get Esperanza.
    B. Alfonso has found Esperanza's missing money orders.
    C. The twins are sick and he needs her to nurse them back to health.
    D. Alfonso has received a message from Miguel asking him to bring Esperanza to the bus station at three o'clock.

3. Who gets off the bus with Miguel?
    A. Tio Marco
    B. Abuelita
    C. Marisol
    D. Tio Luis

4. What does Esperanza finally finish making?
    A. Abuelita's shawl
    B. Flan
    C. A yarn doll for Isabel
    D. Abuelita's blanket

5. A few days before Esperanza's birthday, she begs Miguel to drive her to the foothills before sunrise. Why?
    A. She wants to lie down on the ground to listen to the earth's heartbeat.
    B. She loves to see the sunrise there.
    C. It is her tradition to visit the foothills on the morning of her birthday.
    D. She wants to visit her father's grave.

6. What is Esperanza's birthday surprise?
    A. Papa's roses finally bloom.
    B. Abuelita's arrives from Mexico.
    C. Mama's is released from the hospital.
    D. Miguel, Alfonso, and Juan serenade her with the birthday song.

ANSWER KEY: STUDY QUESTIONS *Esperanza Rising*

	1	2	3	4	5	6	7	8	9	10
1	C	D	A	D	D	C	C	A	B	A
2	D	C	D	A	A	D	D	A	C	D
3	C	C	D	C	C	A	B	C	A	B
4	B	B	B	A	D	C	C	C	D	D
5	B	A	B	A	D	A	C	B	A	A
6	B	B	A	B	A	D	A	B	C	D
7	A	D	A			C			D	
8	C	B				C			A	
9	D	C								
10		D								

VOCABULARY WORKSHEETS

VOCABULARY ASSIGNMENT 1 *Esperanza Rising*

Part I: Using Prior Knowledge and Contextual Clues

Below are the sentences in which the vocabulary words appear in the text. Read the sentence. Use any clues you can find in the sentence combined with your prior knowledge, and write what you think the underlined words mean on the lines provided.

1. And then she felt it. Softly at first. A gentle thumping. Then stronger. A <u>resounding</u> thud, thud, thud against her body.

   _____

2. The short blade was curved like a <u>scythe</u>, its fat wooden handle fitting snugly in her palm.

   _____

3. It had taken every day of three weeks to put the harvest to bed and now everyone <u>anticipated</u> the celebration.

   _____

4. Tomorrow was her birthday and she knew that she would be <u>serenaded</u> at sunrise. Papa and the men who lived on the ranch would congregate below her window, their rich, sweet voices singing *Las Mananitas*, the birthday song.

   _____

5. They both knew that even though it was 1930 and the revolution in Mexico had been over for ten years, there was still <u>resentment</u> against the large landowners.

   _____

6. But Esperanza loved her more for her <u>capricious</u> ways than for her propriety. Abuelita might host a group of ladies for a formal tea in the afternoon, then after they had gone, be found wandering barefoot in the grapes, with a book in her hand, quoting poetry to the birds.

   _____

7. He had the same dark skin and small stature as Hortensia, and Esperanza thought his round eyes, long eyelids, and droopy mustache made him look like a <u>forlorn</u> puppy. He was anything but sad, though.

   _____

8. They tried to pass the time with small talk but their words <u>dwindled</u> into silence.

   _____

9. It wasn't until the candelabra held nothing but short stubs of <u>tallow</u> that Mama finally said, "I see a lantern. Someone is coming!"

   _____

Esperanza Rising Vocabulary Worksheet Assignment 1 Continued

Part II: Determining the Meaning -- Match the vocabulary words to their dictionary definitions.

____ 1. RESOUNDING   A. Made smaller or less

____ 2. SCYTHE   B. Making an echoing sound

____ 3. ANTICIPATED   C. Tending to change abruptly without apparent reason

____ 4. SERENADED   D. Tool with a long, single-edged blade set at an angle on a long, curved handle, used in cutting long grass, grain, etc. by hand

____ 5. RESENTMENT   E. Solid fat taken from animals; used in making candles, soaps, lubricants, etc.

____ 6. CAPRICIOUS   F. Lonely and sad; unhappy and neglected

____ 7. FORLORN   G. Looked forward to; expected

____ 8. DWINDLED   H. Entertained with a vocal or instrumental performance of music outdoors at night, esp. by a lover under the window of his sweetheart

____ 9. TALLOW   I. Feeling of displeasure from a sense of being injured or offended

VOCABULARY ASSIGNMENT 2 *Esperanza Rising*

Part I: Using Prior Knowledge and Contextual Clues

Below are the sentences in which the vocabulary words appear in the text. Read the sentence. Use any clues you can find in the sentence combined with your prior knowledge, and write what you think the underlined words mean on the lines provided.

1. Papa and his vaqueros had been <u>ambushed</u> and killed while mending a fence on the farthest reaches of the ranch.

   _____

2. In front of the adults, Esperanza modeled Mama's refined manners, accepting Marisol's <u>condolences</u>. But as soon as they could, the two girls excused themselves and went to Esperanza's room where they sat on her bed, held hands, and wept as one.

   _____

3. The house was full of visitors and their polite murmurings during the day. Mama was <u>cordial</u> and attentive to everyone, as if entertaining them gave her purpose.

   _____

4. "Your uncles are very powerful and <u>corrupt</u>," said Alfonso. "They can make things difficult for anyone who tries to help you. Remember, they are the banker and the mayor."

   _____

5. A sudden breeze carried a familiar, <u>pungent</u> smell.

   _____

6. They were numb, as if encased in a thick skin that nothing could <u>penetrate</u>.

   _____

7. Avoiding the smoldering piles, she picked through the black wood, hoping to find something to <u>salvage</u>.

   _____

8. "We are <u>indebted</u> to them for our finances and our future. And that trunk of clothes for the poor? Esperanza, it is for us."

   _____

9. Esperanza held a <u>valise</u> filled with clothes, a small package of tamales, and her doll from Papa.

   _____

10. She hurried after Mama, knowing that she might never come back to her home again, and her heart filled with <u>venom</u> for Tio Luis.

    _____

Esperanza Rising Vocabulary Worksheet Assignment 2 Continued

Part II: Determining the Meaning -- Match the vocabulary words to their dictionary definitions.

____ 1. AMBUSHED   A. Attacked from a hidden position

____ 2. CONDOLENCES   B. Expressions of sympathy for a person who is suffering sorrow, misfortune, or grief

____ 3. CORDIAL   C. Pierce or pass into or through

____ 4. CORRUPT   D. Small piece of luggage

____ 5. PUNGENT   E. Guilty of dishonest practices; untrustworthy

____ 6. PENETRATE   F. Friendly; warm

____ 7. SALVAGE   G. Owing for favors or kindness received

____ 8. INDEBTED   H. Saving something from fire, danger, etc.

____ 9. VALISE   I. Poison

____ 10. VENOM   J. Sour or biting smell or taste

VOCABULARY ASSIGNMENT 3 *Esperanza Rising*

Part I: Using Prior Knowledge and Contextual Clues

Below are the sentences in which the vocabulary words appear in the text. Read the sentence. Use any clues you can find in the sentence combined with your prior knowledge, and write what you think the underlined words mean on the lines provided.

1. "They were renegades who thought they had permission to steal from the rich and give to the poor."

   _____

2. The persistent smell of the guavas filled their noses.

   _____

3. He was mesmerized by the locomotive, watching it slowly pull in.

   _____

4. The men and women dressed in their hats and fancy clothes smiled and chuckled at what must have looked like a doting father and two privileged children.

   _____

5. The locomotive arrived pulling a line of cars and hissing and spewing steam.

   _____

6. For hours, Esperanza watched the undulating land pass in front of her.

   _____

7. "When you scorn these people, you scorn Miguel, Hortensia, and Alfonso. And you embarrass me and yourself. As difficult as it is to accept, our lives are different now."

   _____

8. The song of the locomotive was monotonous as they traveled north, and the hours seemed like Mama's never-ending ball of thread unwinding in front of them.

   _____

Esperanza Rising Vocabulary Worksheet Assignment 3 Continued

Part II: Determining the Meaning -- Match the vocabulary words to their dictionary definitions.

____ 1. RENEGADES A. Having a wave-like or rippled form or surface

____ 2. PERSISTENT B. Outlaws; rebels

____ 3. MESMERIZED C. Being excessively fond

____ 4. DOTING D. Determined; refusing to give up

____ 5. SPEWING E. Shooting out forcefully, usually in an uncontrolled manner

____ 6. UNDULATING F. Treat or regard with disrespect or shame

____ 7. SCORN G. Lacking in variety; boring

____ 8. MONOTONOUS H. Spellbound; fascinated

VOCABULARY ASSIGNMENT 4 *Esperanza Rising*

Part I: Using Prior Knowledge and Contextual Clues
　　Below are the sentences in which the vocabulary words appear in the text. Read the sentence. Use any clues you can find in the sentence combined with your prior knowledge, and write what you think the underlined words mean on the lines provided.

1. Inside, the air was <u>stagnant</u> and thick with the smell of body odor.
   _____

2. Esperanza and Mama, their faces shiny with grime and perspiration, looked tired and <u>wilted</u> and they slumped with even the slight weight of their valises.
   _____

3. Mama's <u>demeanor</u> changed. She stood up straight and tall and deliberately blotted her face with a handkerchief.
   _____

4. The old <u>jalopy</u> rocked and swayed as it climbed out of the San Fernando Valley, weaving up through hills covered with dried-out shrubs.
   _____

5. She felt as if she were falling, <u>careening</u> through the hot air.
   _____

6. She stared at the dark brown and purple ridges staggered in the distance and let the ripe tears <u>cascade</u> down her cheeks.
   _____

7. "<u>Strike</u>?" said Miguel. "You mean you will stop working? Don't you need your job?"
   _____

8. Hadn't he seen her rudeness? She <u>brooded</u> as they rode past miles of young tamarisk trees that seemed to be the border of someone's property.
   _____

Esperanza Rising Vocabulary Worksheet Assignment 4 Continued

Part II: Determining the Meaning -- Match the vocabulary words to their dictionary definitions.

____ 1. STAGNANT   A. Rush down in large amounts

____ 2. WILTED   B. Conduct; behavior; manner

____ 3. DEMEANOR   C. Was in a state of gloomy, serious thought

____ 4. JALOPY   D. Limp; drooped; sagging or falling over

____ 5. CAREENING   E. Refuse to do work because of an argument or disagreement with an employer over payment or working conditions

____ 6. CASCADE   F. Wobbling or swerving while in motion, usually at a high speed

____ 7. STRIKE   G. Not flowing or running, as water, air, etc.

____ 8. BROODED   H. Falling apart automobile

VOCABULARY ASSIGNMENT 5 *Esperanza Rising*

Part I: Using Prior Knowledge and Contextual Clues
    Below are the sentences in which the vocabulary words appear in the text. Read the sentence. Use any clues you can find in the sentence combined with your prior knowledge, and write what you think the underlined words mean on the lines provided.

1. "We're lucky," said Isabel solemnly. "In some camps, we had to go in ditches."

    _____

2. The back room had another mattress big enough for two people and a tiny cot.

    _____

3. "Juan went to a lot of trouble to make sure we had this cabin waiting for us when we got here. Please be grateful for the favors bestowed upon us."

    _____

4. Esperanza had never seen Mama wear her hair that way. It was always done up in her beautiful plaited bun, or when she was ready for bed, brushed out and flowing.

    _____

5. A truck piled high with produce drove by, losing a cloud of debris.

    _____

6. Several more onion trucks passed by, their smell accosting her eyes and nose as much as the diapers.

    _____

7. After a few seconds, she gingerly lifted the diaper from the water.

    _____

8. She retrieved the broom and stepped onto the wooden floor.

    _____

Esperanza Rising Vocabulary Worksheet Assignment 5 Continued

Part II: Determining the Meaning -- Match the vocabulary words to their dictionary definitions.

____ 1. SOLEMNLY   A. Remains of anything broken down or destroyed; ruins; rubble

____ 2. COT   B. Presented as a gift; given

____ 3. BESTOWED   C. A light portable bed, esp. one of canvas on a folding frame

____ 4. PLAITED   D. Braided

____ 5. DEBRIS   E. Recovered or regained

____ 6. ACCOSTING   F. With great care or caution

____ 7. GINGERLY   G. Causing serious mood

____ 8. RETRIEVED   H. Approach boldly or aggressively

VOCABULARY ASSIGNMENT 6 *Esperanza Rising*

Part I: Using Prior Knowledge and Contextual Clues

Below are the sentences in which the vocabulary words appear in the text. Read the sentence. Use any clues you can find in the sentence combined with your prior knowledge, and write what you think the underlined words mean on the lines provided.

1. It had been set on its side, forming a little shrine around a plastic statue of Our Lady of Guadalupe.

   _____

2. Esperanza quickly dropped her arms and remembered Marta's taunting voice saying, "No one will be waiting on you here."

   _____

3. Hortensia came over, put her arm around Esperanza and said, "We are accustomed to doing things a certain way, aren't we, Esperanza? But I guess I am not too old to change."

   _____

4. Esperanza continued, reliving the extravagant moments, but was relieved when she knew that Isabel was asleep. For some reason, after hearing about Marta and her family, she felt guilty talking about the richness of her life in Aguascalientes.

   _____

5. "I know a little, but only a few stitches," said Esperanza, remembering Abuelita's blanket of zigzag rows that she had been too preoccupied to unpack.

   _____

6. Lupe was good-natured and less demanding, but Esperanza learned to watch her closely, as she often tried to wander away. If she turned her back for a minute, Esperanza found herself frantically searching for Lupe.

   _____

7. The babies finally fell asleep, drowsy from the heavy air.

   _____

8. "Once the body fights off the infection, it doesn't get it again. For those who live here most of their lives, they are naturally immunized."

   _____

Esperanza Rising Vocabulary Worksheet Assignment 6 Continued

Part II: Determining the Meaning -- Match the vocabulary words to their dictionary definitions.

____ 1. SHRINE   A. Tending towards extreme or excessive spending

____ 2. TAUNTING   B. Teasing

____ 3. ACCUSTOMED   C. Characterized by rapid and disordered or nervous activity

____ 4. EXTRAVAGANT   D. Sleepy

____ 5. PREOCCUPIED   E. Completely lost in thought

____ 6. FRANTICALLY   F. Being in the habit of

____ 7. DROWSY   G. Structure or place blessed or devoted to some saint, holy person, or god, as an altar, chapel, church, or temple

____ 8. IMMUNIZED   H. Protected from a disease

VOCABULARY ASSIGNMENT 7 *Esperanza Rising*

Part I: Using Prior Knowledge and Contextual Clues

Below are the sentences in which the vocabulary words appear in the text. Read the sentence. Use any clues you can find in the sentence combined with your prior knowledge, and write what you think the underlined words mean on the lines provided.

1. She bent over her work, <u>intent</u>, and when her hair fell into her lap, she picked it up and wove it into the blanket.

   _____

2. Women in the camp brought her extra <u>skeins</u> of yarn and Esperanza didn't care that they didn't match.

   _____

3. "It is a lot of strain on her body to <u>cope</u> with so many emotions in such a short time."

   _____

4. They passed miles of naked grapevines, stripped of their harvest and <u>bereft</u> of their leaves.

   _____

5. The dishes were chipped and the blankets <u>frayed</u> and no amount of beating could remove their musty smell.

   _____

6. She turned toward the wall, <u>yearning</u> for the holidays of her past, and repeated what was becoming a nightly ritual of silent tears.

   _____

7. A woman hurried by, carrying a poinsettia plant and wearing a beautiful red wool coat with a rhinestone Christmas tree pinned to the <u>lapel</u>.

   _____

8. Esperanza's eyes <u>riveted</u> on the coat and the jewelry. She wished she could give Mama a warm red coat and a pin that sparkled.

   _____

Esperanza Rising Vocabulary Worksheet Assignment 7 Continued

Part II: Determining the Meaning -- Match the vocabulary words to their dictionary definitions.

____ 1.   INTENT   A.   Worn away or tattered along the edges

____ 2.   SKEINS   B.   Without or lacking

____ 3.   COPE   C.   Continuation of a collar down the front of a coat or shirt

____ 4.   BEREFT   D.   Sharply focused on something

____ 5.   FRAYED   E.   Lengths of thread or yarn wound in loose, long coils

____ 6.   YEARNING   F.   Face and deal with responsibilities, problems, or difficulties

____ 7.   LAPEL   G.   Unsatisfied desire

____ 8.   RIVETED   H.   Fastened (the eye, attention, etc.) firmly to something

VOCABULARY ASSIGNMENT 8 *Esperanza Rising*

Part I: Using Prior Knowledge and Contextual Clues

Below are the sentences in which the vocabulary words appear in the text. Read the sentence. Use any clues you can find in the sentence combined with your prior knowledge, and write what you think the underlined words mean on the lines provided.

1. Esperanza's breath made smoky <u>vapors</u> in front of her face as she waited for the truck to take her to tie grapevines.

   _____

2. She followed along with others, and tied the canes on the <u>taut</u> wire that was stretched post to post.

   _____

3. But she had loved for her to rinse them because afterward, Esperanza would take Mama's hands and put the palms on her own face so she could feel their <u>suppleness</u> and breathe in the fresh smell.

   _____

4. She missed her way of walking into a room, graceful and <u>regal</u>.

   _____

5. "This disease, Valley Fever, makes the body tired and <u>susceptible</u> to other infections."

   _____

6. She was polite enough, answering everyone's questions with the simplest answers, but she was <u>tormented</u> by Mama's absence.

   _____

7. Esperanza <u>reluctantly</u> nodded, remembering the last time they'd given her a lift, but she opened the door.

   _____

8. Esperanza could not stop looking. She felt hypnotized by the <u>squalor</u> but Marta and her mother didn't seem the least bit embarrassed.

   _____

Esperanza Rising Vocabulary Worksheet Assignment 8 Continued

Part II: Determining the Meaning -- Match the vocabulary words to their dictionary definitions.

____ 1. VAPORS   A. Condition of filth and misery

____ 2. TAUT   B. Flexibility

____ 3. SUPPLENESS   C. Visible breath, as fog, mist, steam, smoke, or gas

____ 4. REGAL   D. Experiencing intense pain, especially mental pain

____ 5. SUSCEPTIBLE   E. Easily influenced; weak

____ 6. TORMENTED   F. Unwillingly; disinclined

____ 7. RELUCTANTLY   G. Tightly drawn; tense

____ 8. SQUALOR   H. Grand; fit for royalty

VOCABULARY ASSIGNMENT 9 *Esperanza Rising*

Part I: Using Prior Knowledge and Contextual Clues

Below are the sentences in which the vocabulary words appear in the text. Read the sentence. Use any clues you can find in the sentence combined with your prior knowledge, and write what you think the underlined words mean on the lines provided.

1. When they arrived at the sheds, a crowd of women erupted into shouting and booing.

   _____

2. When Esperanza saw their menacing faces, she wanted to run back to the safety of the camp, do laundry, clean diapers, anything but this.

   _____

3. Esperanza and the other women watched the despondent faces in the windows disappear.

   _____

4. Esperanza lay in bed that night and listened to the others in the front room talk about the sweeps and the deportations.

   _____

5. Esperanza left her there, devoutly praying, and went into the cabin.

   _____

6. As she thought about Papa, tears sprang from her eyes and she suddenly felt weary, as if she had been clinging to a rope but didn't have the strength to hold on any longer.

   _____

7. "I don't want to hear your optimism about this land of possibility when I see no proof!"

   _____

8. "Please remember, though, that once she goes home, she will have to rest to build up her strength. There is still a chance of a relapse.

   _____

Esperanza Rising Vocabulary Worksheet Assignment 9 Continued

Part II: Determining the Meaning -- Match the vocabulary words to their dictionary definitions.

____ 1. ERUPTED   A. Tired

____ 2. MENACING   B. Emerged violently

____ 3. DESPONDENT   C. Lawful removal of illegal immigrants

____ 4. DEPORTATIONS   D. Depressed; gloomy

____ 5. DEVOUTLY   E. Threatening to cause evil, harm, or injury

____ 6. WEARY   F. Characteristic in which someone looks on the more positive side of events or conditions and expects the most positive outcome

____ 7. OPTIMISM   G. Return of a disease or illness after partial recovery from it

____ 8. RELAPSE   H. Expressing devotion or faith

VOCABULARY ASSIGNMENT 10 *Esperanza Rising*

Part I: Using Prior Knowledge and Contextual Clues

Below are the sentences in which the vocabulary words appear in the text. Read the sentence. Use any clues you can find in the sentence combined with your prior knowledge, and write what you think the underlined words mean on the lines provided.

1. A few weeks later, Esperanza stood on the shed dock in the morning and <u>marveled</u> at the peaches, plums, and nectarines that poured into the shed.

   _____

2. Her clothes looked <u>mussed</u> from travel, but she had her same white lace handkerchief tucked into the sleeve of her dress and her eyes brimmed with tears.

   _____

3. After they pulled into camp, they <u>escorted</u> Abuelita into their cabin where they found Josefina, Juan, and the babies waiting.

   _____

4. She could see Mama <u>reclining</u> in the shade near the wooden table.

   _____

5. Esperanza watched Abuelita walk to where Mama slept, resting on the <u>makeshift</u> lounge.

   _____

6. Esperanza listened to Abuelita tell Mama about how <u>infuriated</u> Tio Luis had been when he found out they were gone.

   _____

7. She swooped over Papa's rose blooms, <u>buoyed</u> by rosehips that remembered all the beauty they had seen.

   _____

8. Then she flew over a river, a thrusting <u>torrent</u> that cut through the mountains.

   _____

Esperanza Rising Vocabulary Worksheet Assignment 10 Continued

Part II: Determining the Meaning -- Match the vocabulary words to their dictionary definitions.

____ 1. MARVELED   A. Something made from whatever materials are available, rather than usual means

____ 2. MUSSED   B. Looked at with wonder, admiration, or shock

____ 3. ESCORTED   C. Stream of water flowing with great speed, force, and violence

____ 4. RECLINING   D. Went along with to protect or aid

____ 5. MAKESHIFT   E. Heartened or inspired; uplifted

____ 6. INFURIATED   F. Messy or untidy; rumpled

____ 7. BUOYED   G. Leaning back

____ 8. TORRENT   H. Very angry

VOCABULARY ANSWER KEY - *Esperanza Rising*

	1	2	3	4	5	6	7	8	9	10
1	B	A	B	G	G	G	D	C	B	B
2	D	B	D	D	C	B	E	G	E	F
3	G	F	H	B	B	F	F	B	D	D
4	H	E	C	H	D	A	B	H	C	G
5	I	J	E	F	A	E	A	E	H	A
6	C	C	A	A	H	C	G	D	A	H
7	F	H	F	E	F	D	C	F	F	E
8	A	G	G	C	E	H	H	A	G	C
9	E	D								
10		I								

DAILY LESSONS

LESSON ONE

Objectives

1. To introduce the *Esperanza Rising* unit
2. To discuss proverbs
3. To discuss the two main themes of *Esperanza Rising*
4. To try to predict the plot of *Esperanza Rising*
5. To distribute books, study guides, and other related materials
6. To introduce the Journal Project

Activity One

After the dedication page, the author has included two Mexican proverbs: "He who falls today may rise tomorrow" and "The rich person is richer when he becomes poor, than the poor person when he becomes rich." Write these two proverbs on the board. First, have students work with a partner to create a definition of a proverb (a short saying that expresses a basic truth). When a definition has been established, ask students again to work with a partner to decide what basic truths are being expressed in these two proverbs. Discuss as a class. Finally, explain to students that these two proverbs are closely related to the main themes of *Esperanza Rising*. Have students predict what the story is going to be about based upon the proverbs and the title of the book. (You may consider showing the cover of the book so that students can also base their predictions upon the cover illustration). Consider posting the predictions on the bulletin board.

Activity Two

Distribute the materials students will use in this unit. Explain in detail how students are to use these materials.

Study Guides

Students should read the study guide questions for each reading assignment prior to beginning the reading assignment to get a feeling for what events and ideas are important in the section they are about to read. After reading the section, students will (as a class or individually) answer the questions to review the important events and ideas from that section of the book. Students should keep the study guides as study materials for the unit test.

Vocabulary

Prior to each reading assignment, students will do vocabulary work related to the section of the book they are about to read. Following the completion of the reading of the book, there will be a vocabulary review of all the words used in the vocabulary assignments. Students should keep their vocabulary work as study materials for the unit test.

Reading Assignment Sheet

You need to fill in the Reading Assignment Sheet to let students know by when their reading has to be completed. You can either write the assignment sheet up on the side blackboard or bulletin board and leave it there for students to see each day, or you can make copies for each student to have. In either case, you should advise students to become very familiar with the reading assignments so they know what is expected of them.

Extra Activities Center

The Unit Resource Materials portion of this LitPlan contains suggestions for an extra library of related books and articles in your classroom as well as crossword and word search puzzles. Make an extra activities center in your room where you will keep these materials for students to use. (Bring the books and articles in from the library and keep several copies of the puzzles on hand.)

Explain to students that these materials are available for students to use when they finish reading assignments or other class work early.

Non-fiction Assignment Sheet
Explain to students that they each are to read at least one non-fiction piece from the in-class library at some time during the unit. Students will fill out a Non-fiction Assignment Sheet after completing the reading to help you (the teacher) evaluate their reading experiences and to help the students think about and evaluate their own reading experiences.

Books
Each school has its own rules and regulations regarding student use of school books. Advise students of the procedures that are normal for your school. Preview the book. Look at the covers, front matter, and index.

Activity Three
Distribute the Journal Project Sheet. Discuss directions in detail. If your school has the resources available, you may want to acquire notebooks for each student to use as a journal. Otherwise, students may acquire their own notebooks or type their journals.

JOURNAL PROJECT SHEET *Esperanza Rising*

PROMPT
The novel *Esperanza Rising* is about a thirteen year-old girl who must leave her aristocratic home in Aguascalientes, Mexico and travel to California to work as a farm laborer. The story is told from the third-person point of view by an omniscient narrator. But what if it were told from the first-person point of view by one of the characters? Your assignment is to create a journal with at least twenty entries in which you retell the story from the view point of one of the characters.

GETTING STARTED
Obtain a new notebook that you will be using as your journal (unless your teacher tells you differently). Create a list of your favorite characters. Although Esperanza is the protagonist, there are many strong minor characters like Miguel, Mama, and Isabel. Whose eyes do you think you could see through the best?

Be creative: include illustrations or decorate your journal.

REQUIREMENTS
You must have at least 20 entries and your entries must cover the entire story from beginning to end. You must write at least two paragraphs per entry and you must write from the first person point of view as one of the characters.

LESSON TWO

Objectives
1. To preview the study questions and vocabulary from Assignment 1
2. To read Assignment 1
3. To give students practice reading orally
4. To evaluate students' oral reading
5. To discuss the use of foreshadowing
6. To discuss the use of and create a metaphor

Activity One
Preview the study questions together orally as a class.

Activity Two
Complete the vocabulary worksheet for Assignment 1 orally together as a class. Discuss and post the answers so all students have the correct answers to study.

Activity Three
Have students read Assignment 1 of *Esperanza Rising* orally in class. You probably know the best way to choose readers with your class: pick students at random, ask for volunteers, or use whatever method works best for your group. If you have not yet completed an oral reading evaluation for your students this marking period, this would be a good opportunity to do so. A form is included with this unit for your convenience.

Activity Four
Discuss the definition of foreshadowing with students. Ask students to find an example of foreshadowing in the chapter "Las Uvas" (Esperanza pricks her finger with the rose).
The finger-pricking scene is layered with symbolism (the rose could be Papa or Esperanza and the thorn could be Tio Luis). This might be a good opportunity to discuss symbolism as well. Discuss the reasons why the author decided to forewarn the reader. Ask students if the foreshadowing adds suspense or interest to the story.

Activity Five
Esperanza tells Miguel that there is a deep river that runs between them. Explain to students that this is a metaphor explaining Esperanza's relationship with Miguel. Have students decide on the definition for a metaphor and explain what this metaphor means.

Have students create a metaphor in which they describe a special relationship in their own lives. Consider posting the metaphors on the bulletin board.

ORAL READING EVALUATION
Esperanza Rising

Name _____ Class _____ Date _____

SKILL	EXCELLENT	GOOD	AVERAGE	FAIR	POOR
FLUENCY	5	4	3	2	1
CLARITY	5	4	3	2	1
AUDIBILITY	5	4	3	2	1
PRONUNCIATION	5	4	3	2	1
_____	5	4	3	2	1
_____	5	4	3	2	1
_____	5	4	3	2	1

Total Grade:

Comments:

LESSON THREE

Objectives
1. To review the main events and ideas from Assignment 1
2. To discuss the significance of the title "Las Uvas" and the symbolism of grapes
3. To preview the study questions and vocabulary for Assignment 2
4. To read Assignment 2
5. To give students practice reading orally
6. To evaluate students' oral reading

Activity One
Give students a few minutes to formulate answers for the study guide questions for Assignment 1 and then discuss the answers to the questions in detail. Write the answers on the board or overhead transparency so students can have the correct answers for study purposes.

NOTE: It is good practice in public speaking and leadership skills for individual students to take charge of leading the discussions of the study questions. Perhaps a different student could go to the front of the class and lead the discussion each day that the study questions are discussed in this unit. Of course, you should guide the discussion when appropriate and try to fill in any gaps students may leave. The study questions could really be handled in a number of different ways, including in small groups with group reports following. Occasionally you may want to use the multiple choice questions as quizzes to check students' reading comprehension. As a short review now and then, students could pair up for the first (or last, if you have time left at the end of a class period) few minutes of class to quiz each other from the study questions. Mix up methods of reviewing the materials and checking comprehension throughout the unit so students don't get bored just answering the questions the same way each day. Variety in methods will also help address the different learning styles of your students.

From now on in this unit the directions will simply say, "Discuss the answers to the study questions as previously directed." You will choose the method of preparation and discussion each day based on what best suits you and your class.

Activity Two
Distribute copies of the Fruits and Vegetables Worksheet. You will be using this worksheet for every reading assignment so make sure to have enough copies on hand.

Fruits and vegetables play an important role in Esperanza's story. In fact, the title of each chapter is named after a fruit or vegetable. Assignment 1 included a chapter entitled "Las Uvas" and therefore today's discussion will revolve around grapes.

Bring in a bunch of grapes and distribute one grape per student. Instruct students not to eat the grape until they have reached the "What does it taste like?" section. Have them eat the grape slowly and truly reflect on the flavor. Using their powers of observation and the text, students will fill out the worksheet. Discuss their answers and the symbolism/importance of grapes in the text.

Consider posting the best worksheets on the bulletin board.

NOTES:
In this activity and others like it that follow, be aware and considerate of possible food allergies your students may have.

As an alternative, divide the class into 12 groups. Each group will taste a different fruit and complete the worksheet for each reading assignment. Post worksheets on the bulletin board for all students to view.

This activity is repeated for each reading assignment. Rather than writing out this whole explanation each time, future directions will say, "Do the Fruit and Vegetable Worksheet for [name of fruit or vegetable] as previously directed."

Activity Three
Give students time to preview the study questions and do the vocabulary work for Assignment 2. Discuss the answers to the vocabulary worksheets.

Activity Four
Continue the oral reading evaluations while reading Assignment 2 in class. If this reading assignment is not completed in class, tell students they should complete this reading assignment prior to the next class.

FRUIT AND VEGETABLE WORKSHEET *Esperanza Rising*

Name _____ Date _____

Name of Fruit or Vegetable _____

I. What does it look like?

II. What does it smell like?

III. What does it taste like?

IV. What does it make you think of? Do you have a special memory that comes to mind?

V. Where does it appear in the text? (quotations)

VI. What does it symbolize? Why is it important to the story?

LESSON FOUR

Objectives
1. To review the main events and ideas from Assignment 2
2. To discuss the significance of the chapter titles "Las Papayas" and "Los Higos"
3. To preview the study questions for Assignment 3
4. To preview the study questions and vocabulary for Assignment 3
5. To have students research and read non-fiction related to the book
6. To read Assignment 3

Activity One
Discuss the answers to the study questions for Assignment 2 as previously directed. While students have their study guides out, preview the questions for Assignment 3.

Activity Two
Distribute the Fruit and Vegetable Worksheet for "Las Papayas" and "Los Higos."
Do the Fruit and Vegetable Worksheet for figs and papayas as previously directed.
Give students a sample of both a fig and papaya in order to complete their worksheets.
Discuss their responses and the significance of papayas and figs in the text.

Activity Three
Ask students to identify the metaphor Abuelita uses for Esperanza's need to overcome life's challenges (the Phoenix rising from the ashes). Discuss.

Have students create a metaphor for a time when they had to overcome a difficulty in life. Ask for students who would like to share their metaphors.

Activity Four
Take students to the library/media center to find articles, books, etc. about non-fiction topics related to *Esperanza Rising*. Suggested topics include: the Mexican Revolution, the Great Depression, migrant workers, California agriculture, California's produce industry, Mexico, the Mexican culture, Cesar Chavez, "Okies," etc. In Lesson 15, students will give an oral report on their non-fiction topics. There is also a list of Related Topics in the Unit Resources section of this LitPlan.

Activity Five
Tell students that prior to the next class meeting they should review the study questions, complete the vocabulary work, and read Assignment 3. Inform students they will be giving an oral presentation on their topic.

NON-FICTION ASSIGNMENT SHEET
(To be completed after reading the required non-fiction article)

Name _____ Date _____

Title of Non-fiction Read _____

Written By _____ Publication Date _____

I. Factual Summary: Write a short summary of the piece you read.

II. Vocabulary
    1. With which vocabulary words in the piece did you encounter some degree of difficulty?

    2. How did you resolve your lack of understanding with these words?

III. Interpretation: What was the main point the author wanted you to get from reading his work?

IV. Criticism
    1. With which points of the piece did you agree or find easy to accept? Why?

    2. With which points of the piece did you disagree or find difficult to believe? Why?

V. Personal Response: What do you think about this piece? OR How does this piece influence your ideas?

LESSON FIVE

Objectives
1. To review the main events, ideas, and vocabulary from Assignment 3
2. To discuss the significance of the title "Las Guayabas"
3. To preview the study questions and vocabulary for Assignment 4
4. To read Assignment 4

Activity One
Discuss the answers to the study questions for Assignment 3 as previously directed. While students have their study guides out, preview the questions for Assignment 4.

Activity Two
Review the vocabulary from Assignment 3. Then, give students time to do the vocabulary work for Assignment 4.

Activity Three
Do the Fruit and Vegetable Worksheet for "Las Guayabas" as previously directed.

Activity Four
Have students read Assignment 4 orally in class.

If students do not finish reading Assignment 4 in class, they should do so prior to the next class meeting.

If you have finished the oral reading evaluations, students may read silently.

LESSON SIX

Objectives
1. To review the main events, ideas, and vocabulary from Assignment 4
2. To discuss the significance of the chapter title "Los Melones" and the importance of cantaloupes in the text
3. To discuss conflict in literature
4. To preview the study questions and vocabulary for Assignment 5
5. To read Assignment 5

Activity One
Discuss the answers to the study questions for Assignment 4 as previously directed. While students have their study guides out, preview the questions for Assignment 5.

Activity Two
Do the Fruit and Vegetable Worksheet for "Los Melones" as previously directed.

Activity Three
Distribute the Conflict Type Worksheet.

Explain to students there are many different kinds of conflicts: Character vs. Character, Character vs. Self, Character vs. Nature, and Character vs. Society. Discuss the meaning of each type of conflict. Have students brainstorm examples of each kind of conflict. Students should think not only about other stories they may have read in school, but also television shows and movies they may have seen. For example, they may think of Harry Potter vs. Lord Voldemort as a type of Character vs. Character conflict.

Have students complete the Conflict Type Worksheet for *Esperanza Rising*. When they finish, discuss the conflicts they have noted on their worksheets. Encourage students to hold onto their charts and fill in the conflicts as they progress through the book. You may want to keep a class log of the conflicts on the bulletin board.

Activity Four
Discuss the answers to the vocabulary worksheet for Assignment 4. Do the vocabulary work for Assignment 5 orally together in class.

Activity Five
Students should read Assignment 5 silently during the remaining class time. If they do not finish reading Assignment 5 in class, they should do so prior to the next class meeting.

CONFLICT TYPE WORKSHEET *Esperanza Rising*

Name _____ Date _____

I. Character vs. Character

II. Character vs. Nature

III. Character vs. Self

IV. Character vs. Society

LESSON SEVEN

Objectives
1. To review the main events, ideas, and vocabulary from Assignment 5
2. To discuss the significance of the title "Las Cebollas" and the symbolism of onions in the text
3. To preview the study questions and vocabulary for Assignment 6
4. To read Assignment 6

Activity One
Discuss the answers to the study questions for Assignment 5 as previously directed. While students have their study guides out, preview the questions for Assignment 6.

Activity Two
Discuss the answers to the vocabulary worksheet for Assignment 5. Do the vocabulary work for Assignment 6 orally together in class.

Tell students to read Assignment 6 prior to the next class meeting. If they finish the following writing assignment early, they may begin the reading assignment in class.

Activity Three
Do the Fruit and Vegetable Worksheet for "Las Cebollas" as previously directed. You may want to introduce the idea of an onion as a metaphor for the layers in a character's personality (each layer of the onion represents a different facet of the character). Also, the shedding of the onions in the text could represent the shedding of Esperanza's privileged life.

Activity Four
Distribute Writing Assignment #1 and discuss the directions in detail. Give students the remainder of the period to work on the assignment. Assign a due date and decide on a length for the composition.

WRITING ASSIGNMENT 1 *Esperanza Rising*

PROMPT
Esperanza Rising is about a young woman who leaves her familiar surroundings and is placed in an environment that is totally unfamiliar to her. This new environment poses many challenges for Esperanza and ultimately leads to a change in her attitude.

Your assignment is to write a narrative about a time when you were removed from a familiar environment and thrust into a new one. Describe your world before, during, and after the change. Remember, your narrative needs to have a beginning, middle, and end.

PREWRITING
Did you change schools? Did you move from one house to another? Did you visit a foreign country? Perhaps you visited a friend or relative for a week or two. Think about the times you had to change or adapt to a new environment. Choose a time that had the greatest impact on you. Make notes about your world "before," "during," and "after" the change took place. Write down words, phrases, and incidents that characterize each period as well as words and phrases that express how you felt at each stage. How did it all turn out? Make a few notes about the outcome.

DRAFTING
There are many ways to begin writing a story. The important thing is to hook your reader. Use descriptive language (lots of adjectives) to help your reader understand the place, time, and mood of your story. Think about some of your favorite books and try to remember how the author hooked you into reading that particular story. Some books start in the middle of the action. Some start with a description of the setting. Some start with dialogue. Choose your opening and begin writing. Make sure you use the first person to narrate your story. If you include dialogue, don't forget to use quotation marks and begin a new paragraph when a new character begins speaking. Follow the notes that you made in the pre-writing step above. In your first draft, just get your ideas on paper. Then, go back and refine your organization and your writing. Make your writing interesting with descriptive words and phrases, and double-check your grammar, spelling, and punctuation.

PROMPT
When you finish the rough draft of your narrative, ask a student who sits near you to read it. After reading your rough draft, he/she should tell you what he/she liked best about your work, which parts were difficult to understand, and ways in which your work could be improved. Reread your paper considering your critic's comments, and make the corrections you think are necessary. Ask your classmate what he/she thought of each of the characters/events you chose for your assignment.

Do a final proofreading of your paper double-checking your grammar, spelling, organization, and the clarity of your ideas, and prepare a final copy.

FINAL DRAFT
Follow your teacher's directions for making a final copy of your report.

WRITING EVALUATION FORM *Esperanza Rising*

Name _____ Date _____

Grade _____

Circle One For Each Item:

Grammar: correct errors noted on paper

Spelling: correct errors noted on paper

Punctuation: correct errors noted on paper

Legibility: excellent   good   fair   poor

_____ excellent   good   fair   poor

_____ excellent   good   fair   poor

Strengths:

Weaknesses:

Comments/Suggestions:

LESSON EIGHT

Objectives
1. To review the main events and ideas from Assignment 6
2. To discuss the significance of the chapter titles "Las Almendras" and "Las Ciruelas"
3. To analyze the rose metaphor in Assignment 6
4. To preview the study questions and vocabulary for Assignment 7
5. To read Assignment 7

Activity One
Discuss the answers to the study questions for Assignment 6 as previously directed. While students have their study guides out, preview the questions for Assignment 7.

Activity Two
Do the Fruit and Vegetable Worksheet for "Las Almendras" and "Las Ciruelas" as previously directed. Could the almond with its hard exterior and soft interior be a symbol for one of the characters?

Activity Three
In "Las Almendras," Miguel and Alfonso show Esperanza the rose they secretly brought with them from Mexico. Is the rose a metaphor for Esperanza's character? Discuss with the class. Refer to "Las Papayas" to see when the rose was first mentioned.

Activity Four
Give students time to do the vocabulary work for Assignment 7. When students finish, discuss the answers to the vocabulary worksheet for Assignment 7.

Activity Five
Students should read Assignment 7 silently. Instruct students to finish reading Assignment 7 prior to the next class meeting.

LESSON NINE

Objectives
1. To review the main events and ideas from Assignment 7
2. To discuss the significance of the chapter title "Las Papas" and the symbolism of potatoes in the text
3. To preview the study questions and vocabulary for Assignment 8
4. To read Assignment 8
5. To evaluate students' writing skills through writing conferences
6. To revise Writing Assignment #1 based on the teacher's suggestions

Activity One
Discuss answers to the study questions for Assignment 7 as previously directed. While students have their study guides out, preview the questions for Assignment 8.

Activity Two
Do the Fruit and Vegetable Worksheet for "Las Papas" as previously directed.
Discuss student responses. Could the eyes of the potatoes represent growth and new beginnings?

Activity Three
Do the vocabulary work for Assignment 8 orally together in class.

Activity Four
Have students read Assignment 8 silently while you conduct writing conferences with each student for Writing Assignment #1. Be sure to advise students when the final copy of the writing assignment is due.

LESSON TEN

Objectives
1. To review the main events and ideas from Assignment 8
2. To discuss the significance of the chapter title "Los Aguacates" and the symbolism of avocados in the text
3. To preview the study questions and vocabulary for Assignment 9
4. To read Assignment 9
5. To practice persuasive writing
6. To examine two different points of view
7. To determine and support one's own point of view after examining an issue

Activity One
Discuss the answers to the study questions for Assignment 8 as previously directed. While students have their study guides out, preview the questions for Assignment 9.

Activity Two
Do the Fruit and Vegetable Worksheet for "Los Aguacates" as previously directed.

Activity Three
Give students time to do the vocabulary work for Assignment 9. After students finish, discuss the answers to the vocabulary worksheets.

Tell students to read Assignment 9 prior to the next class meeting. If they complete the writing assignment early, they may begin reading in class.

Activity Four
Distribute Writing Assignment #2 and discuss the directions in detail. Give students the remainder of the period to work on the assignment. Assign a due date.

WRITING ASSIGNMENT #2 *Esperanza Rising*

PROMPT
In *Esperanza Rising*, there are two different "camps" of farm laborers: those who want to strike for better salaries and living conditions and those who don't want to strike because they fear losing their jobs or being deported to Mexico. Do you agree with Marta who fights for better conditions for all Mexican workers? Or do you agree with Esperanza who is simply trying to help her family. Your assignment is to write a persuasive essay in which you argue for or against striking.

PREWRITING
Reasons For/Benefits Of Striking (Marta's Side):
[Include page numbers where these reasons/benefits are mentioned or implied in the text.]

_____

_____

_____

_____

_____

Reasons Against Striking (Esperanza's Side):
[Include page numbers where these reasons are mentioned or implied in the text.]

_____

_____

_____

_____

_____

Decide which side you think is right--whether the workers should strike or not.

DRAFTING
Write an introductory paragraph in which you introduce the idea that some workers (like Marta) want to strike but others (like Esperanza) do not, and give your opinion as to whether or not you think the workers should strike.

Choose the two best reasons offered as to why the workers should (or should not, depending on your view) strike. Write one paragraph about each reason (two separate paragraphs) using details from the story to support your points.

Write a concluding paragraph in which you mention a few of the other miscellaneous reasons that support your viewpoint and bring your "argument" to a close.

PROMPT

When you finish the rough draft, ask someone whose opinion you trust to read it. After reading your rough draft, he/she should tell you what he/she liked best about your work, which parts were difficult to understand, and ways in which your work could be improved. Reread your paper considering your critic's comments and make the corrections you think are necessary.

PROOFREADING

Do final proofreading of your paper double-checking your grammar, spelling, organization, and the clarity of your ideas, then make a final copy.

LESSON ELEVEN

Objectives
1. To review the main events and ideas from Assignment 9
2. To discuss the significance of the chapter titles "Los Esparragos" and "Los Duraznos"
3. To discuss the zigzag pattern metaphor
4. To preview the study questions and vocabulary for Assignment 10
5. To read Assignment 10

Activity One
Discuss study questions for Assignment 9 as previously directed. While students have their study guides out, preview the questions for Assignment 10.

Activity Two
Do the Fruit and Vegetable Worksheet for "Los Esparragos" and "Los Duraznos" as previously directed.

Activity Three
Discuss the zigzag pattern Esperanza uses as a metaphor for her life in the camp.

Then, have students create a metaphor for their own lives and another metaphor for what they want their lives to be like in the future.

Activity Four
Give students time to do the vocabulary work for Assignment 10. When they finish, discuss the answers to the vocabulary worksheet.

Activity Five
Have students read Assignment 10 silently. Tell students to finish reading Assignment 10 prior to the next class meeting.

LESSON TWELVE

Objectives
1. To review the main events and ideas from Assignment 10
2. To discuss the significance of the chapter title "Las Uvas"
3. To assess what students have learned from the novel
4. To evaluate students' writing skills
5. To revise Writing Assignment #2 based on teacher's suggestions
6. To practice writing to inform

Activity One
Discuss the answers to the study questions for Assignment 10 as previously directed.

Activity Two
Have students review their Fruit and Vegetable Worksheet for the first chapter entitled "Las Uvas." Then, have them fill in any new information they have gleaned from the last chapter which is also entitled "Las Uvas."

Activity Three
Distribute Writing Assignment #3. Discuss the directions in detail and give students ample time to complete the assignment. Give students the remainder of the class period to work on this assignment. Determine the amount of time your students will need to complete this assignment to your standards and tell them when the paper will be due.

While students are working on Writing Assignment #3, conduct writing conferences with each student for Writing Assignment #2. Make sure to tell students when to turn in their revised Writing Assignment #2.

WRITING ASSIGNMENT #3 *Esperanza Rising*

PROMPT
The fictional story of *Esperanza Rising* is set against the historical backdrop of the Great Depression and the influx of migrant farm workers into California. There were many families like Esperanza's who were forced to leave their homes and seek jobs working for meager wages as farm laborers and living in humble conditions. Write a response to literature in which you explain what you have learned from reading about Esperanza's experiences.

PREWRITING
Create a list of things you have learned from reading *Esperanza Rising*. Think about what you have learned regarding the Mexican culture, the Great Depression, migrant workers and their camps, labor strikes, immigration, railroad travel, segregation, prejudice, family relationships, and life in general. Look through your list and see which things "go together," perhaps under the topics listed above. Choose two or three topics that have the most items to use as the topics for paragraphs in the body of your composition.

DRAFTING
Write an introductory paragraph in which you state in a sentence or two what the book *Esperanza Rising* is about, then tell that you learned many things from reading it.

In the body of your composition write several paragraphs, one for each of the main topics you had many items for in the prewriting step above. Be sure to use a topic sentence for each paragraph and include the details about what you have learned, citing examples from the book.

Write a concluding paragraph in which you mention other, miscellaneous things you have learned from Esperanza and bring your composition to a close.

PROMPT
When you finish the rough draft, ask someone whose opinions you trust to read it. After reading your rough draft he/she should tell you what he/she liked best about your work, which parts were difficult to understand, and ways in which your work could be improved. Reread your paper considering your critic's comments. Make the corrections you think are necessary.

PROOFREADING
Do a final proofreading of your paper, double-checking your grammar, spelling, organization, and the clarity of your ideas. Then make a final copy.

LESSON THIRTEEN

<u>Objectives</u>
      To review the vocabulary work done in this unit

<u>Activity</u>
Choose one (or more) of the vocabulary review activities listed below and spend your class period as directed in the activity. Some of the materials for these review activities are located in the Vocabulary Resource Materials section in this LitPlan.

VOCABULARY REVIEW ACTIVITIES

1. Divide your class into two teams and have an old-fashioned spelling or definition bee.

2. Give each of your students (or students in groups of two, three, or four) an *Esperanza Rising* Vocabulary Word Search Puzzle. The person (group) to find all of the vocabulary words in the puzzle first wins.

3. Give students an *Esperanza Rising* Vocabulary Word Search Puzzle without the word list. The person or group to find the most vocabulary words in the puzzle wins.

4. Use an *Esperanza Rising* Vocabulary Crossword Puzzle. Put the puzzle onto a transparency on the overhead projector (so everyone can see it), and do the puzzle together as a class.

5. Give students an *Esperanza Rising* Vocabulary Matching Worksheet to do.

6. Divide your class into two teams. Use *Esperanza Rising* vocabulary words with their letters jumbled as a word list. Student 1 from Team A faces off against Student 1 from Team B. Write the first jumbled word on the board. The first student (1A or 1B) to unscramble the word wins the chance for his/her team to score points. If 1A wins the jumble, go to student 2A and give him/her a definition. He/she must give you the correct spelling of the vocabulary word which fits that definition. If he/she does, Team A scores a point, and you give student 3A a definition for which you expect a correctly spelled matching vocabulary word. Continue giving Team A definitions until some team member makes an incorrect response. An incorrect response sends the game back to the jumbled-word face off, this time with students 2A and 2B. Instead of repeating giving definitions to the first few students of each team, continue with the student after the one who gave the last incorrect response on the team. For example, if Team B wins the jumbled-word face-off, and student 5B gave the last incorrect answer for Team B, you would start this round of definition questions with student 6B, and so on. The team with the most points wins!

7. Have students write a story in which they correctly use as many vocabulary words as possible. Have students read their compositions orally. Post the most original compositions on your bulletin board.

LESSONS FOURTEEN AND FIFTEEN

<u>Objectives</u>
1. To discuss the ideas and themes from *Esperanza Rising* in greater detail
2. To exercise critical thinking skills
3. To review for the unit test

<u>Activity One</u>
Choose the questions from the Extra Discussion Questions/Writing Assignments which seem most appropriate for your students. A class discussion of these questions is most effective if students have been given the opportunity to formulate answers to the questions prior to the discussion. To this end, you may either have all the students formulate answers to all the questions, divide your class into groups and assign one or more questions to each group, or you could assign one questions to each student in your class. The option you choose will make a difference in the amount of class time needed for this activity.

<u>Activity Two</u>
After students have had ample time to formulate answers to the questions, begin your class discussion of the questions and the ideas presented by the questions. Be sure students take notes during the discussion so they have another resource to study for the test.

EXTRA DISCUSSION QUESTIONS *Esperanza Rising*

Interpretive

1. Where is the climax of the story? Justify your answer.
2. What are two main conflicts in the story? Explain each fully.
3. What is the main setting of the story? Is there more than one? How important is the setting to the story? Explain.
4. What are two main themes in the story? List events or passages from the story that support each.

Critical

5. Why do you think Mama says, "You will feel differently as you get older" when Esperanza declares she will marry Miguel? What does Mama's response reveal about the Mexican culture during this time period?
6. Find at least three instances of foreshadowing in the first two chapters of the book. What is revealed? Why do you think the author chose to forewarn the reader?
7. What does the scene in which Esperanza and her father lie down to hear the heartbeat of the earth reveal about their relationship?
8. What does Esperanza mean when she says to Miguel that there is a "deep river" that runs between them?
9. Compare and contrast the Ortega family with Alfonso's family.
10. What does the following quotation reveal about Tio Luis: "Ramona, grieving does not suit you. I hope you will not wear black all year!"?
11. Miguel races into the burning house to save Abuelita. What does this reveal about his character?
12. Compare Papa to Tio Luis and Tio Marco.
13. What does the story of Miguel, the mouse, and the house thieves reveal about his character?
14. What does Esperanza's reaction to the train car and the peasants reveal about her character?
15. Esperanza and Miguel take a train ride together when they are children. Compare and contrast this train ride with the one they take after fleeing El Rancho de las Rosas.
16. Compare Esperanza's experience of listening to the earth in "Los Melones" with the parallel experience in "Aguascalientes, Mexico." What has changed? How does she react? Why?
17. Describe Esperanza's first encounter with Marta. What does the encounter reveal about Marta's character? What does it reveal about Esperanza's character?
18. Describe the landscape Esperanza sees in California. How does this compare and contrast to the familiar landscape of Mexico?
19. When the women are taking a bath, Esperanza runs to get hot water for Hortensia before anyone else could. Why does she do this? What does it show about her transformation?
20. How is Esperanza's life different at the camp than in Mexico?
21. What does Esperanza teach Isabel to do? What does this reveal about the growth of her character?
22. Esperanza becomes determined to finish Abuelita's blanket after Mama gets sick. Why? Of what is the blanket symbolic?

23. What does Alfonso mean when he tells Miguel that Mr. Yakota is "getting rich on other people's bad manners"?
24. Esperanza and Miguel see Esperanza's pinata hanging from a tree in the strikers' camp. What does the pinata symbolize?
25. Compare and contrast the two chapters entitled "Las Uvas." Why does the author begin and end the book with chapters bearing the same title?
26. Why can't Esperanza hear the earth's heartbeat in "Los Melones" but she can hear it at the end of the book in "Las Uvas"? What has changed?
27. In the last chapter, Esperanza finishes Abuelita's blanket. What is the significance of this? What significance does crocheting have in the book as a whole? How would the book have been different if crocheting had not been incorporated?
28. How does Esperanza change throughout the story and how does her development reflect the author's main themes?
29. Esperanza's name means "hope." How is she a hopeful character? What is the meaning of the title of the book?
30. Compare and contrast Esperanza and Marta.
31. Compare and contrast Esperanza and Isabel.
32. How are Esperanza and her family impacted by segregation and discrimination?

Critical/Personal Response

33. Why do you think the first chapter isn't named after a fruit or vegetable like all the other chapters?
34. When Miguel and Esperanza were young children, Papa planted a rose for each of them. Describe the rose planted for Esperanza and the one planted for Miguel. How do these roses reflect their personalities? Why do you think Papa planted them right next to each other?
35. Why do you think the immigration official seems "angry for no reason" when speaking to Mama? What does his behavior reveal about the social class system in 1930s Mexico?
36. Compare Mama's and Esperanza's reactions to their new lives. Who would you most resemble if you were in the same situation?
37. Compare the strikers' camp to the camp in which Esperanza lives. How is Esperanza affected by the strikers' camp? Did reading about the camp affect you? How?
38. Miguel says that there will be a time in the future when they "will have to decide all over again whether to join" the strikers or not. Do you think Miguel and the others should join the strikers in the future? Why or why not? Would you have joined the strikers if you had been in the same position? Why or why not?
39. If you were in Miguel's shoes, would you have dug ditches? Do you agree with Esperanza when she says Miguel is letting his boss at the railroad take advantage of him? Why or why not?
40. Do you agree with Miguel when he tells Esperanza that she has never lived without hope? Why or why not?
41. Why do you think the author uses the names of fruits and vegetables as the titles of the book's chapters?
42. Do you know anyone who acts like Marta? How are they alike and how are they different?

43. Who is the hero of the story? Is it Miguel because he brings back Abuelita? Is it Esperanza because she earns the money to pay for Abuelita's voyage? Justify your answer.

Personal Response

44. Do you agree with Mama's decision to leave Mexico instead of marrying Tio Luis? Would you have made the same decision? Why or why not?
45. Esperanza and Mama are forced to live in a cabin with several other people. How would you and your family react in a similar situation? Would your relationships get stronger or weaker? Explain your answer.
46. Esperanza is embarrassed by her lack of knowledge and she's afraid the others at the camp will laugh at her. Isabel tells her that it is best to just face people and to laugh if she gets teased. Describe a situation where you have been embarrassed. How did you handle it? Did you laugh it off? Why or why not?
47. At the beginning of "Las Uvas," Esperanza thinks Miguel has betrayed her. Have you ever been betrayed by a friend or relative? Describe the experience. How did you feel? What did you do?
48. At the end of "Las Uvas," Esperanza tells Isabel, "Do not be afraid to start over." Where else in the book have these words occurred? Have you ever had to start something over again? Describe the experience. How did you feel about starting over? What is difficult? Why or why not?
49. Which character would you like to have as a friend and why?
50. Would you recommend this book to a friend? Why or why not?
51. Have you ever been in a setting like the camp where Esperanza lives? What was it like? If not, would you like to visit such a place? Why?
52. Have you ever been in a setting like El Rancho de las Rosas? What was it like? If not, would you like to visit such a place? Why?

QUOTATIONS *Esperanza Rising*

1. "Wait a little while and the fruit will fall into your hand. You must be patient, Esperanza."

2. She pressed closer to the ground, until her body was breathing with the earth's. And with Papa's. The three hearts beating together.

3. "There is no rose without thorns."

4. "Do not be afraid to start over."

5. Esperanza stood on one side and Miguel stood on the other and the river could never be crossed.

6. At first, they stayed only a few hours, but soon they became like la calabaza, the squash plant in Alfonso's garden, whose giant leaves spread out, encroaching upon anything smaller.

7. "My father and I have lost faith in our country. We were born servants here and no matter how hard we work we will always be servants."

8. "You were right, Esperanza. In Mexico we stand on different sides of the river."

9. "We are like the phoenix. Rising again, with a new life ahead of us."

10. "Papa's heart will find us wherever we go."

11. "I am poor, but I am rich. I have my children, I have a garden with roses, and I have my faith and the memories of those who have gone before me. What more is there?"

12. "The rich take care of the rich and the poor take care of those who have less than they have."

13. But Papa's influence was gone. What would happen to Miguel's dreams now?

14. "There is a Mexican saying: 'Full bellies and Spanish blood go hand in hand.'"

15. "So you're a princess who's come to be a peasant? Where's all your finery?"

16. "Here, we have two choices. To be together and miserable or to be together and happy... I choose to be happy. So which will you choose?"

17. He smiled and pointed to the one that was closest to the cabin wall and already had a makeshift trellis propped against it. "So you can climb," he said.

18. The mountains and valleys in the blanket were easy. But as soon as she reached a mountain, she was headed back down into a valley again. Would she ever escape this valley she was living in?

19. Her other life seemed like a story she had read in a book a long time ago, un cuento de hadas, a fairy tale.

20. "Esperanza, people here think that all Mexicans are alike. They think that we are all uneducated, dirty, poor, and unskilled."

21. "Americans see us as one big brown group who are good for only manual labor."

22. The strikers only listened if you agreed with them.

23. "In Mexico, I was a second-class citizen. I stood on the other side of the river, remember? And I would have stayed that way my entire life. At least here, I have a chance, however small, to become more than what I was."

24. When Esperanza told Abuelita their story, about all that had happened to them, she didn't measure time by the usual seasons. Instead, she told it as a field-worker, in spans of fruits and vegetables and by what needed to be done to the land.

25. Miguel had been right about never giving up, and she had been right, too, about rising above those who held them down.

26. He who falls today may rise tomorrow.

27. The rich person is richer when he becomes poor, than the poor person when he becomes rich.

28. "See these perfect rows, Miguel? They are like what my life would have been. These rows know where they are going. Straight ahead. Now my life is like the zigzag in the blanket on Mama's bed."

LESSON SIXTEEN

Objectives
1. To widen the breadth of students' knowledge about topics related to the novel
2. To check students' non-fiction reading assignments

Activity One

Ask each student to give a brief oral report about the non-fiction articles he/she read. Your criteria for evaluating this report will vary depending on the level of your students. You may wish for students to give a complete report without using notes of any kind, or you may want students to read directly from a written report, or you may want to do something in between these two extremes. Just make students aware of your criteria in ample time for them to prepare their reports.

Start with one student's report. After each report, ask if anyone else in the class has read about a topic related to the first student's report. If no one has, choose another student at random. After all reports on a topic are given, take a minute to hold a short class discussion about the information students have just heard.

LESSON SEVENTEEN

Objectives
> To review the main ideas and events in *Esperanza Rising*

Activity
Choose one of the review games/activities suggested below and spend your class time as directed in the activity.

REVIEW GAMES/ACTIVITIES

1. Ask the class to make up a unit test for *Esperanza Rising*. The test should have four sections: matching, true/false, short answer, and essay. Students may use 1/2 the period to make the test and then swap papers and use the other 1/2 of the period to take a test a classmate has devised. You may want to use the unit test included in this packet or take questions from the students' test to formulate your own test.

2. Take 1/2 the period for students to make up true and false questions (including answers). Collect the papers and divide the class into two teams. Draw a big tic-tac-toe board on the chalk board. Make one team X and one team O. Ask questions to each side, giving each student one turn. If the question is answered correctly, that students' team's letter (X or O) is placed in the box. IF the answer is incorrect, no letter is place in the box. The object is to get three in a row like tic-tac-toe. You may want to keep track of the number of games won for each team.

3. Take 1/2 the period for students to make up questions (true/false and short answer). Collect the questions. Divide the class into two teams. You'll alternate asking questions to individual members of teams A and B (like in a spelling bee). The question keeps going from A to B until it is correctly answered, then a new question is asked. A correct answer does not allow the team to get another question. Correct answers are +2 points; incorrect answers are -1 point.

4. Have students pair up and quiz each other from their study guides and class notes.

5. Give students an *Esperanza Rising* crossword puzzle to complete.

6. Divide your class into two teams. Use the *Esperanza Rising* unit word list. Student 1 from Team A faces off against Student 1 form Team B. You write the first jumbled word on the board. The first student (1A or 1B) to unscramble the word wins the chance for his/her team to score points. If 1A wins the jumble, go to student 2A and give him/her a clue. He/she must give you the correct word which matches that clue. If he/she does, Team A scores a point, and you give student 3A a clue for which you expect another correct response. Continue giving Team A clues until some team member makes an incorrect response. An incorrect response sends the game back to the jumbled-word face off, this time with students 2A and 2B. Instead of repeated giving clues to the first few students of each team, continue with the student after the one who gave the last incorrect response on the team. For example, if Team B wins the jumbled-word face-off, and student 5B gave the last incorrect answer for Team B, you would start this round of clue questions with student 6B, and so on. The team with the most points wins!

7. Play "What's My Line?". This is similar to the old television show. Students assume the roles of different characters from the story. One student gives clues to the class, or to a panel of contestants. The contestants try to guess the identity of the guest. Students may enjoy assisting you in creating rules and procedures for the game.

8. Play Jeopardy. Divide the class into two groups. Assign each group a category or chapter

from the story and have them devise answers for that category. Play the game according to the television show procedures.

9. Play Drawing in the Details. This is similar to Pictionary. Divide students into teams. A student from one team draws a scene from the story. (You may want to specify the chapter.) Drawings should be kept simple, to keep the pace lively. Students in the opposing team locate the scene in their books and read it aloud. If they are incorrect, the illustrator's team has a chance to guess. Involve students in setting up a scoring system and any other necessary rules.

LESSON EIGHTEEN

<u>Objectives</u>
To test the students' understanding of the main ideas and themes in *Esperanza Rising*

<u>Activity</u>
Distribute the unit tests. Give students ample time to complete them and collect the tests when students finish. Remember to collect assigned books prior to the end of the class period (and any other assignments that haven't yet been turned in!).

NOTE: There are 5 different unit tests included in this LitPlan Teacher Pack. Two are short answer and two are multiple choice. There is one advanced short answer test. The answers to the advanced short answer test will be based on the discussions you have had in class and should be graded accordingly. You should choose the tests and/or test parts which best suit your needs. Matching and short answer tests have answer keys. For essay type questions, grade according to your own criteria based on class discussions and the level of your students. Also, you will need to choose vocabulary words to read orally for the vocabulary sections of the short answer tests.

UNIT TESTS

Esperanza Rising Short Answer Unit Test 1

I. Matching

____ 1.	ABUELITA	A.	Esperanza's last name
____ 2.	ALFONSO	B.	What Isabel wants for Christmas
____ 3.	MIGUEL	C.	Bought for Mama but given to the campesino family at the strikers' camp
____ 4.	LUIS	D.	They hide dangerous "surprises" in the harvest.
____ 5.	CARMEN	E.	Author of *Esperanza Rising*
____ 6.	RAMONA	F.	Gives Mama two hens for her future; the "egg lady"
____ 7.	SWEEPING	G.	Miguel's nickname for Esperanza
____ 8.	ARVIN	H.	Esperanza's maternal grandmother
____ 9.	REINA	I.	Wants to marry Mama
____ 10.	MARTA	J.	Esperanza's job at the camp when she first arrives
____ 11.	JUAN	K.	Esperanza's father
____ 12.	PINATA	L.	Isabel's mother
____ 13.	STRIKERS	M.	Boy Esperanza declared she would marry one day
____ 14.	SIXTO	N.	Wants the workers to band together and strike
____ 15.	ORTEGA	O.	Esperanza's mother
____ 16.	JOSEFINA	P.	Hortensia's husband and Miguel's father
____ 17.	RYAN	Q.	Metaphor Abuelita uses to describe how they will overcome their troubles
____ 18.	PLUMS	R.	Cause the twins to become ill
____ 19.	PHOENIX	S.	Setting of the camp where Esperanza and Mama live and work in California
____ 20.	ANYTHING	T.	Isabel's father

II. Short Answer

1. Why do Papa and Esperanza lie flat on the ground?

2. Who are Tio Luis and Tio Marco? What do they bring to Mama the night Papa is late coming home?

3. Who is responsible for setting fire to El Rancho de las Rosas?

4. How does Esperanza feel about riding in the train car from Zacatecas?

5. Why does Esperanza become upset when the family stops for lunch on their way to the camp?

6. Why doesn't Esperanza want to go to the jamaica?

7. Why does the doctor recommend that Mama to go to the hospital?

8. What are the living conditions at the strikers' camp?

9. What luxuries will the new camp for the workers from Oklahoma have?

10. What is Esperanza's birthday surprise?

III. Composition
1. Esperanza's name means "hope." How is she a hopeful character? What is the meaning of the title of the book?

IV. Vocabulary
    A. Write the vocabulary words you are given. After writing them down, go back and write in their definitions.

Word	Definition
1	
2	
3	
4	
5	
6	
7	
8	
9	
10	

Esperanza Rising Short Answer Unit Test 1 Answer Key

I. Matching

H	1.	ABUELITA	A.	Esperanza's last name
P	2.	ALFONSO	B.	What Isabel wants for Christmas
M	3.	MIGUEL	C.	Bought for Mama but given to the campesino family at the strikers' camp
I	4.	LUIS	D.	They hide dangerous "surprises" in the harvest.
F	5.	CARMEN	E.	Author of *Esperanza Rising*
O	6.	RAMONA	F.	Gives Mama two hens for her future; the "egg lady"
J	7.	SWEEPING	G.	Miguel's nickname for Esperanza
S	8.	ARVIN	H.	Esperanza's maternal grandmother
G	9.	REINA	I.	Wants to marry Mama
N	10.	MARTA	J.	Esperanza's job at the camp when she first arrives
T	11.	JUAN	K.	Esperanza's father
C	12.	PINATA	L.	Isabel's mother
D	13.	STRIKERS	M.	Boy Esperanza declared she would marry one day
K	14.	SIXTO	N.	Wants the workers to band together and strike
A	15.	ORTEGA	O.	Esperanza's mother
L	16.	JOSEFINA	P.	Hortensia's husband and Miguel's father
E	17.	RYAN	Q.	Metaphor Abuelita uses to describe how they will overcome their troubles
R	18.	PLUMS	R.	Cause the twins to become ill
Q	19.	PHOENIX	S.	Setting of the camp where Esperanza and Mama live and work in California
B	20.	ANYTHING	T.	Isabel's father

II. Short Answer

1. Why do Papa and Esperanza lie flat on the ground?
   Papa tells Esperanza that when one lies down on the land, one can feel it breathe and its heart beating. He is explaining to Esperanza that the whole valley breathes and lives. Esperanza wants to experience this, so Papa has her lie flat on the ground next to him with her cheek pressed against the earth.

2. Who are Tio Luis and Tio Marco? What do they bring to Mama the night Papa is late coming home?
   They are Papa's older stepbrothers. Tio Luis is the bank president and Tio Marco is the mayor of the town. They bring Mama the silver belt buckle that belongs to Papa--a sign that something bad may have happened to him.

3. Who is responsible for setting fire to El Rancho de las Rosas?
   Tio Luis and Tio Marco are responsible for the fire.

4. How does Esperanza feel about riding in the train car from Zacatecas?
   She does not want to travel in the car because it is not clean and the people do not look trustworthy to her.

5. Why does Esperanza become upset when the family stops for lunch on their way to the camp?
   Esperanza becomes upset because she can't hear the heartbeat of the valley like she could at El Rancho de las Rosas.

6. Why doesn't Esperanza want to go to the jamaica?
   She is embarrassed because the whole camp knows she doesn't know how to sweep. She also doesn't want to see Marta who ridiculed her for not knowing how to sweep.

7. Why does the doctor recommend that Mama to go to the hospital?
   The doctor says Mama is not getting any better, and she is depressed. He thinks she needs nursing around the clock in order to get well.

8. What are the living conditions at the strikers' camp?
   There are ten toilets for hundreds of people. Some people live in tents but others only have burlap bags stretched between poles. The kitchens are outdoors. In an irrigation ditch, women are washing clothes and children are bathing at the same time. Clotheslines run everywhere.

9. What luxuries will the new camp for the workers from Oklahoma have?
   The new camp will have toilets and hot water inside the cabins and a swimming pool.

10. What is Esperanza's birthday surprise?
    Miguel, Alfonso, and Juan serenade her with the birthday song.

IV. Vocabulary
    A. Write the vocabulary words you are given. After writing them down, go back and write in their definitions.

Word	Definition
1	
2	
3	
4	
5	
6	
7	
8	
9	
10	

Select the vocabulary words for Short Answer Test 1.

Esperanza Rising Short Answer Unit Test 2

I. Matching

____ 1. HORTENSIA   A. Esperanza's housekeeper

____ 2. QUINCEANERA   B. Lupe and Pepe

____ 3. DOLL   C. Contains a statue of Our Lady of Guadalupe

____ 4. MARISOL   D. Esperanza's new friend who helps watch the twins

____ 5. PAPA   E. Wants to be the Queen of May

____ 6. ISABEL   F. Isabel's father

____ 7. RAMONA   G. Made by Josefina to sell at the jamaica

____ 8. TWINS   H. Abuelita's sisters who help Mama and Esperanza get their traveling papers

____ 9. REINA   I. Marta's mother

____ 10. MARTA   J. Esperanza's father

____ 11. FLAN   K. Papa's last gift to Esperanza

____ 12. JUAN   L. Mayor of Aguascalientes

____ 13. MELINA   M. Promised Miguel he would help him get a job on the railroad one day

____ 14. YAKOTA   N. Wants the workers to band together and strike

____ 15. ADA   O. Esperanza has to cut these off the potatoes

____ 16. EYES   P. A presentation party that girls have when they turn fifteen in Mexico

____ 17. GROTTO   Q. Esperanza's best friend

____ 18. MARCO   R. Miguel's nickname for Esperanza

____ 19. SIXTO   S. Market owner who is kind to Mexicans

____ 20. NUNS   T. Esperanza's mother

II. Short Answer

1. What job does Esperanza do that is typically reserved for the eldest son of a wealthy rancher?

2. What event is Esperanza looking forward to that takes place three weeks after the harvest?

3. How does Papa die?

4. Who helps Mama and Esperanza obtain traveling papers and clothes?

5. Why is Esperanza shocked that Mama is telling Carmen "the egg woman" about their troubles?

6. Why do Esperanza and Mama have to share a cabin with Hortensia and Alfonso?

7. Esperanza tells Mama that she will pray for many things in church, but what does she pray for most of all?

8. Marta's aunt shares some news that causes the working women to worry. What is the news?

9. What happens to Miguel that causes everyone in the cabin to celebrate?

10. What special present does Esperanza give to Isabel? Why?

III. Quotations: Explain the importance and meaning of the following quotations:

1. "Do not be afraid to start over."

2. "Papa's heart will find us wherever we go."

3. "There is a Mexican saying: 'Full bellies and Spanish blood go hand in hand.'"

4. The mountains and valleys in the blanket were easy. But as soon as she reached a mountain, she was headed back down into a valley again. Would she ever escape this valley she was living in?

5. He who falls today may rise tomorrow.

IV. Composition
1. What are two main themes in the story? List events or passages from the story that support each.

V. Vocabulary
    A. Write the vocabulary words you are given. After writing them down, go back and write in their definitions.

Word	Definition
1	
2	
3	
4	
5	
6	
7	
8	
9	
10	

Esperanza Rising Short Answer Unit Test 2 Answer Key

I. Matching

A	1.	HORTENSIA	A.	Esperanza's housekeeper
P	2.	QUINCEANERA	B.	Lupe and Pepe
K	3.	DOLL	C.	Contains a statue of Our Lady of Guadalupe
Q	4.	MARISOL	D.	Esperanza's new friend who helps watch the twins
M	5.	PAPA	E.	Wants to be the Queen of May
E	6.	ISABEL	F.	Isabel's father
T	7.	RAMONA	G.	Made by Josefina to sell at the jamaica
B	8.	TWINS	H.	Abuelita's sisters who help Mama and Esperanza get their traveling papers
R	9.	REINA	I.	Marta's mother
N	10.	MARTA	J.	Esperanza's father
G	11.	FLAN	K.	Papa's last gift to Esperanza
F	12.	JUAN	L.	Mayor of Aguascalientes
D	13.	MELINA	M.	Promised Miguel he would help him get a job on the railroad one day
S	14.	YAKOTA	N.	Wants the workers to band together and strike
I	15.	ADA	O.	Esperanza has to cut these off the potatoes
O	16.	EYES	P.	A presentation party that girls have when they turn fifteen in Mexico
C	17.	GROTTO	Q.	Esperanza's best friend
L	18.	MARCO	R.	Miguel's nickname for Esperanza
J	19.	SIXTO	S.	Market owner who is kind to Mexicans
H	20.	NUNS	T.	Esperanza's mother

II. Short Answer

1. What job does Esperanza do that is typically reserved for the eldest son of a wealthy rancher?
   Esperanza cuts the first bunch of grapes with a special knife signaling the beginning of the harvest season.

2. What event is Esperanza looking forward to that takes place three weeks after the harvest?
   She is looking forward to the fiesta that celebrates both the end of the harvest season and her birthday.

3. How does Papa die?
   Papa and his vaqueros are ambushed and killed by bandits while mending a fence on the farthest reaches of the ranch.

4. Who helps Mama and Esperanza obtain traveling papers and clothes?
   Abuelita's sisters help Mama and Esperanza. Because they are nuns, they are able to obtain the items very discreetly without Tio Luis finding out.

5. Why is Esperanza shocked that Mama is telling Carmen "the egg woman" about their troubles?
   Esperanza is shocked because when they lived in Aguascalientes, Mama would have said it was inappropriate to tell an "egg woman" their problems. Mama explains to Esperanza that it is all right to tell their problems to peasants because they are now peasants too.

6. Why do Esperanza and Mama have to share a cabin with Hortensia and Alfonso?
   They have to share a cabin because at this family camp there is no housing for single women. The landowner will only give one cabin for each man and his family.

7. Esperanza tells Mama that she will pray for many things in church, but what does she pray for most of all?
   She will pray that Abuelita will get well, that she will be able to get her money from Tio Luis's bank, and that she will soon join Mama and Esperanza in California.

8. Marta's aunt shares some news that causes the working women to worry. What is the news?
   She tells the women that the Mexicans who do not strike might be in danger. They may be harmed by those who do strike.

9. What happens to Miguel that causes everyone in the cabin to celebrate?
   Miguel gets a new job working for the railroad.

10. What special present does Esperanza give to Isabel? Why?
    Esperanza gives Isabel her porcelain doll because Isabel was not chosen as the Queen of May.

V. Vocabulary
  A. Write the vocabulary words you are given. After writing them down, go back and write in their definitions.

Word	Definition
1	
2	
3	
4	
5	
6	
7	
8	
9	
10	

Select the vocabulary words for Short Answer Test 2.

Esperanza Rising Multiple Choice Unit Test 1

I. Matching

____ 1.	HORTENSIA	A.	Pattern in Abuelita's blanket
____ 2.	ALFONSO	B.	Market owner who is kind to Mexicans
____ 3.	DOLL	C.	Esperanza's new friend who helps watch the twins
____ 4.	MARISOL	D.	Working there is Miguel's dream job.
____ 5.	JAMAICAS	E.	Esperanza puts this on her hands to make them soft again
____ 6.	MARTA	F.	Hortensia's husband and Miguel's father
____ 7.	AGUASCALIENTES	G.	Location of El Rancho de las Rosas
____ 8.	PATRONA	H.	Wants the workers to band together and strike
____ 9.	MELINA	I.	Spanish for "head of the household"
____ 10.	YAKOTA	J.	Given to Esperanza by Abuelita with the instructions to finish it while waiting for Abuelita to join them in California
____ 11.	ZIGZAG	K.	Esperanza's best friend
____ 12.	ROSES	L.	Esperanza's housekeeper
____ 13.	SIXTO	M.	Field-workers
____ 14.	JOSEFINA	N.	Brought to California by Miguel and Alfonso as a surprise for Mama and Esperanza
____ 15.	RAILROAD	O.	Esperanza can feel its heart beating.
____ 16.	BLANKET	P.	Papa's last gift to Esperanza
____ 17.	AVOCADO	Q.	Summer camp parties with music and food held every Saturday night
____ 18.	CAMPESINOS	R.	Destroys the Ortegas' house
____ 19.	FIRE	S.	Isabel's mother
____ 20.	LAND	T.	Esperanza's father

II. Multiple Choice

1. Why do Papa and Esperanza lie flat on the ground?
    A. They are playing a game of hide-and-go-seek.
    B. Esperanza has fallen while cutting the first fruit of the harvest season. Papa bends down to pick her up.
    C. Papa tells Esperanza that the whole valley breathes and lives. She wants to feel the land breathing and hear its heartbeat.
    D. They are attempting to hide from bandits who are angry with Papa.

2. Why do Esperanza and Mama have to share a cabin with Hortensia and Alfonso?
    A. The landowner will only give one cabin for each man and his family; there is no housing for single women.
    B. Mama doesn't want to be separated from her only friends in the United States.
    C. Hortensia and Alfonso need Esperanza to clean the cabin and cook while they are at work.
    D. Mama and Esperanza can't afford the rent for their own cabin.

3. What is Mama's job at the camp?
    A. Mama works in the shed packing grapes.
    B. Mama picks grapes in the fields.
    C. Mama is responsible for sweeping the platform.
    D. Mama is responsible for watching the twins while Josefina is at work.

4. Why doesn't Esperanza want to go to the jamaica?
    A. She doesn't know anyone and is afraid she will be lonely.
    B. She doesn't like to dance.
    C. She doesn't have a pretty dress to wear.
    D. She is embarrassed because the whole camp knows she doesn't know how to sweep.

5. What does Mama say she will pray for?
    A. She prays that Esperanza will be strong, no matter what happens.
    B. She prays that she will someday have dresses like she did in Mexico.
    C. She prays that she will earn enough money to buy a home for herself and Esperanza.
    D. She prays that she will find a husband that can take care of her and her daughter.

6. How does the dust storm affect Mama?
   A. The dust from the storm blinds Mama.
   B. Mama becomes depressed because the storm causes Esperanza to get sick.
   C. Mama loves the storm because it reminds her of Mexico.
   D. Because of the storm, Mama gets Valley Fever.

7. Why does Esperanza start working?
   A. Esperanza starts working because she needs to help Hortensia and Alfonso pay the rent.
   B. Esperanza starts working because she wants to earn money to bring Abuelita to California.
   C. Esperanza starts working because Marta makes fun of her.
   D. Esperanza starts working because she wants to buy a ticket to return to Mexico.

8. How does Esperanza spend her Christmas?
   A. She spends her Christmas on a train to Mexico in hopes of bringing Abuelita to California.
   B. She spends her Christmas packing potatoes in the sheds.
   C. She spends her Christmas with Mama at the hospital.
   D. She spends her Christmas praying in church that Mama will get better.

9. Why do Miguel and Esperanza shop at Mr. Yakota's market when there are other markets much closer to the camp?
   A. Mr. Yakota is a good friend of the family.
   B. Mr. Yakota has discounted prices.
   C. Mr. Yakota is kind to Mexicans and he stocks many of the foods that Mexicans like.
   D. The owners of the farm have a deal with Mr. Yakota and force the workers to shop from his store.

10. Who is Marta?
    A. Marta is Esperanza's grandmother.
    B. Marta is a young girl Esperanza meets on the train.
    C. Marta is a girl about Miguel's age who lives in a camp where they pick cotton.
    D. Marta is the name of the doll Esperanza got from her father.

11. What does Esperanza think the first time she sees Isabel?
    A. She thinks Isabel is a whining crybaby.
    B. She thinks Isabel looks like the doll her father gave her.
    C. She thinks Isabel is a very interesting character, and she wants to have a chance to talk with her about her travels.
    D. She thinks she and Isabel will become best friends.

12. What event occurs that causes Esperanza to think the words, "bad luck"?
    A. She pricks herself with a thorn from a rose while waiting for Papa in the garden.
    B. She has a bad dream about her father.
    C. She finds her father's silver belt-buckle in the vineyard.
    D. Her uncles Luis and Marco arrive for a visit.

13. Who are Alfonso and Miguel?
    A. Alfonso is a field-worker and Miguel is his best-friend.
    B. Alfonso is Hortensia's husband and Miguel is their son.
    C. Alfonso is Esperanza's uncle and Miguel is her cousin.
    D. Alfonso and Miguel are Esperanza's uncles who visit the ranch when Papa goes missing.

14. How does Papa die?
    A. Tio Luis and Tio Marco murder him in his sleep.
    B. Papa and his vaqueros are ambushed and killed by bandits while mending a fence on the farthest reaches of the ranch.
    C. He is killed by a wild animal while fixing the fence on the ranch.
    D. He falls off his horse and is trampled to death.

15. Why doesn't Mama inherit Papa's land upon his death?
    A. The land didn't belong to Papa. Tio Luis really owns the land.
    B. It isn't customary to leave land to women.
    C. Mama is supposed to inherit the land, but Tio Luis and Tio Marco change Papa's will after he dies.
    D. Mama doesn't want to live on the land anymore. It reminds her too much of Papa.

16. Who rescues Abuelita from the house fire?
    A. Tio Luis
    B. Alfonso
    C. Esperanza
    D. Miguel

17. Who helps Mama and Esperanza obtain traveling papers and clothes?
    A. Abuelita's sisters
    B. Senor Rodriguez
    C. Hortensia and Alfonso
    D. Tio Luis and Tio Marco

18. How did Papa reward Miguel for protecting Esperanza when bandits were robbing the house?
    A. Papa gave Miguel a new suit.
    B. Papa gave Miguel money.
    C. Papa treated Miguel to a day-long train ride to Zacatecas.
    D. Papa told Miguel he could one day marry Esperanza.

19. What is Miguel's dream job?
    A. He wants to be the boss of the field-workers like his father.
    B. He wants to own a ranch like Papa some day.
    C. He wants to be in politics like Tio Marco.
    D. He wants to work for the railroad.

20. What happens to Miguel that makes everyone in the cabin celebrate?
    A. Miguel gets a raise.
    B. Miguel gets engaged.
    C. Miguel gets a new job working for the railroad.
    D. Miguel finds a new job in Northern California.

III. Composition
1. How is Esperanza's life different at the camp than in Mexico?

IV. Vocabulary

____ 1. ANTICIPATED   A. Emerged violently
____ 2. FORLORN   B. Being excessively fond
____ 3. RENEGADES   C. Wobbling or swerving while in motion, usually at a high speed
____ 4. PERSISTENT   D. With great care or caution
____ 5. DOTING   E. Threatening to cause evil, harm, or injury
____ 6. CAREENING   F. Looked forward to; expected
____ 7. BROODED   G. Approach boldly or aggressively
____ 8. COT   H. Lawful removal of illegal immigrants
____ 9. ACCOSTING   I. Lonely and sad; unhappy and neglected
____ 10. GINGERLY   J. Was in a state of gloomy, serious thought
____ 11. RETRIEVED   K. Determined; refusing to give up
____ 12. PREOCCUPIED   L. Continuation of a collar down the front of a coat or shirt
____ 13. COPE   M. Messy or untidy; rumpled
____ 14. LAPEL   N. Outlaws; rebels
____ 15. REGAL   O. A light portable bed, esp. one of canvas on a folding frame
____ 16. ERUPTED   P. Grand; fit for royalty
____ 17. MENACING   Q. Face and deal with responsibilities, problems, or difficulties
____ 18. DEPORTATIONS   R. Recovered or regained
____ 19. MUSSED   S. Very angry
____ 20. INFURIATED   T. Completely lost in thought

Esperanza Rising Multiple Choice Unit Test 1 Answer Key

I. Matching

L	1.	HORTENSIA	A.	Pattern in Abuelita's blanket
F	2.	ALFONSO	B.	Market owner who is kind to Mexicans
P	3.	DOLL	C.	Esperanza's new friend who helps watch the twins
K	4.	MARISOL	D.	Working there is Miguel's dream job.
Q	5.	JAMAICAS	E.	Esperanza puts this on her hands to make them soft again
H	6.	MARTA	F.	Hortensia's husband and Miguel's father
G	7.	AGUASCALIENTES	G.	Location of El Rancho de las Rosas
I	8.	PATRONA	H.	Wants the workers to band together and strike
C	9.	MELINA	I.	Spanish for "head of the household"
B	10.	YAKOTA	J.	Given to Esperanza by Abuelita with the instructions to finish it while waiting for Abuelita to join them in California
A	11.	ZIGZAG	K.	Esperanza's best friend
N	12.	ROSES	L.	Esperanza's housekeeper
T	13.	SIXTO	M.	Field-workers
S	14.	JOSEFINA	N.	Brought to California by Miguel and Alfonso as a surprise for Mama and Esperanza
D	15.	RAILROAD	O.	Esperanza can feel its heart beating.
J	16.	BLANKET	P.	Papa's last gift to Esperanza
E	17.	AVOCADO	Q.	Summer camp parties with music and food held every Saturday night
M	18.	CAMPESINOS	R.	Destroys the Ortegas' house
R	19.	FIRE	S.	Isabel's mother
O	20.	LAND	T.	Esperanza's father

II. Multiple Choice

C 1. Why do Papa and Esperanza lie flat on the ground?
   A. They are playing a game of hide-and-go-seek.
   B. Esperanza has fallen while cutting the first fruit of the harvest season. Papa bends down to pick her up.
   C. Papa tells Esperanza that the whole valley breathes and lives. She wants to feel the land breathing and hear its heartbeat.
   D. They are attempting to hide from bandits who are angry with Papa.

A 2. Why do Esperanza and Mama have to share a cabin with Hortensia and Alfonso?
   A. The landowner will only give one cabin for each man and his family; there is no housing for single women.
   B. Mama doesn't want to be separated from her only friends in the United States.
   C. Hortensia and Alfonso need Esperanza to clean the cabin and cook while they are at work.
   D. Mama and Esperanza can't afford the rent for their own cabin.

A 3. What is Mama's job at the camp?
   A. Mama works in the shed packing grapes.
   B. Mama picks grapes in the fields.
   C. Mama is responsible for sweeping the platform.
   D. Mama is responsible for watching the twins while Josefina is at work.

D 4. Why doesn't Esperanza want to go to the jamaica?
   A. She doesn't know anyone and is afraid she will be lonely.
   B. She doesn't like to dance.
   C. She doesn't have a pretty dress to wear.
   D. She is embarrassed because the whole camp knows she doesn't know how to sweep.

A 5. What does Mama say she will pray for?
   A. She prays that Esperanza will be strong, no matter what happens.
   B. She prays that she will someday have dresses like she did in Mexico.
   C. She prays that she will earn enough money to buy a home for herself and Esperanza.
   D. She prays that she will find a husband that can take care of her and her daughter.

D 6. How does the dust storm affect Mama?
- A. The dust from the storm blinds Mama.
- B. Mama becomes depressed because the storm causes Esperanza to get sick.
- C. Mama loves the storm because it reminds her of Mexico.
- D. Because of the storm, Mama gets Valley Fever.

B 7. Why does Esperanza start working?
- A. Esperanza starts working because she needs to help Hortensia and Alfonso pay the rent.
- B. Esperanza starts working because she wants to earn money to bring Abuelita to California.
- C. Esperanza starts working because Marta makes fun of her.
- D. Esperanza starts working because she wants to buy a ticket to return to Mexico.

C 8. How does Esperanza spend her Christmas?
- A. She spends her Christmas on a train to Mexico in hopes of bringing Abuelita to California.
- B. She spends her Christmas packing potatoes in the sheds.
- C. She spends her Christmas with Mama at the hospital.
- D. She spends her Christmas praying in church that Mama will get better.

C 9. Why do Miguel and Esperanza shop at Mr. Yakota's market when there are other markets much closer to the camp?
- A. Mr. Yakota is a good friend of the family.
- B. Mr. Yakota has discounted prices.
- C. Mr. Yakota is kind to Mexicans and he stocks many of the foods that Mexicans like.
- D. The owners of the farm have a deal with Mr. Yakota and force the workers to shop from his store.

C 10. Who is Marta?
- A. Marta is Esperanza's grandmother.
- B. Marta is a young girl Esperanza meets on the train.
- C. Marta is a girl about Miguel's age who lives in a camp where they pick cotton.
- D. Marta is the name of the doll Esperanza got from her father.

B 11.   What does Esperanza think the first time she sees Isabel?
   A.   She thinks Isabel is a whining crybaby.
   B.   She thinks Isabel looks like the doll her father gave her.
   C.   She thinks Isabel is a very interesting character, and she wants to have a chance to talk with her about her travels.
   D.   She thinks she and Isabel will become best friends.

A 12.   What event occurs that causes Esperanza to think the words, "bad luck"?
   A.   She pricks herself with a thorn from a rose while waiting for Papa in the garden.
   B.   She has a bad dream about her father.
   C.   She finds her father's silver belt-buckle in the vineyard.
   D.   Her uncles Luis and Marco arrive for a visit.

B 13.   Who are Alfonso and Miguel?
   A.   Alfonso is a field-worker and Miguel is his best-friend.
   B.   Alfonso is Hortensia's husband and Miguel is their son.
   C.   Alfonso is Esperanza's uncle and Miguel is her cousin.
   D.   Alfonso and Miguel are Esperanza's uncles who visit the ranch when Papa goes missing.

B 14.   How does Papa die?
   A.   Tio Luis and Tio Marco murder him in his sleep.
   B.   Papa and his vaqueros are ambushed and killed by bandits while mending a fence on the farthest reaches of the ranch.
   C.   He is killed by a wild animal while fixing the fence on the ranch.
   D.   He falls off his horse and is trampled to death.

B 15.   Why doesn't Mama inherit Papa's land upon his death?
   A.   The land didn't belong to Papa. Tio Luis really owns the land.
   B.   It isn't customary to leave land to women.
   C.   Mama is supposed to inherit the land, but Tio Luis and Tio Marco change Papa's will after he dies.
   D.   Mama doesn't want to live on the land anymore. It reminds her too much of Papa.

D 16. Who rescues Abuelita from the house fire?
- A. Tio Luis
- B. Alfonso
- C. Esperanza
- D. Miguel

A 17. Who helps Mama and Esperanza obtain traveling papers and clothes?
- A. Abuelita's sisters
- B. Senor Rodriguez
- C. Hortensia and Alfonso
- D. Tio Luis and Tio Marco

C 18. How did Papa reward Miguel for protecting Esperanza when bandits were robbing the house?
- A. Papa gave Miguel a new suit.
- B. Papa gave Miguel money.
- C. Papa treated Miguel to a day-long train ride to Zacatecas.
- D. Papa told Miguel he could one day marry Esperanza.

D 19. What is Miguel's dream job?
- A. He wants to be the boss of the field-workers like his father.
- B. He wants to own a ranch like Papa some day.
- C. He wants to be in politics like Tio Marco.
- D. He wants to work for the railroad.

C 20. What happens to Miguel that makes everyone in the cabin celebrate?
- A. Miguel gets a raise.
- B. Miguel gets engaged.
- C. Miguel gets a new job working for the railroad.
- D. Miguel finds a new job in Northern California.

IV. Vocabulary

F	1.	ANTICIPATED	A.	Emerged violently
I	2.	FORLORN	B.	Being excessively fond
N	3.	RENEGADES	C.	Wobbling or swerving while in motion, usually at a high speed
K	4.	PERSISTENT	D.	With great care or caution
B	5.	DOTING	E.	Threatening to cause evil, harm, or injury
C	6.	CAREENING	F.	Looked forward to; expected
J	7.	BROODED	G.	Approach boldly or aggressively
O	8.	COT	H.	Lawful removal of illegal immigrants
G	9.	ACCOSTING	I.	Lonely and sad; unhappy and neglected
D	10.	GINGERLY	J.	Was in a state of gloomy, serious thought
R	11.	RETRIEVED	K.	Determined; refusing to give up
T	12.	PREOCCUPIED	L.	Continuation of a collar down the front of a coat or shirt
Q	13.	COPE	M.	Messy or untidy; rumpled
L	14.	LAPEL	N.	Outlaws; rebels
P	15.	REGAL	O.	A light portable bed, esp. one of canvas on a folding frame
A	16.	ERUPTED	P.	Grand; fit for royalty
E	17.	MENACING	Q.	Face and deal with responsibilities, problems, or difficulties
H	18.	DEPORTATIONS	R.	Recovered or regained
M	19.	MUSSED	S.	Very angry
S	20.	INFURIATED	T.	Completely lost in thought

Esperanza Rising Multiple Choice Unit Test 2

I. Matching

____ 1. ABUELITA A. Setting of the camp where Esperanza and Mama live and work in California

____ 2. MIGUEL B. Esperanza's last name

____ 3. LUIS C. Bought for Mama but given to the campesino family at the strikers' camp

____ 4. CARMEN D. la Migra; sent the strikers to Mexico

____ 5. RAMONA E. Main crop of El Rancho de las Rosas

____ 6. SWEEPING F. Metaphor Abuelita uses to describe how they will overcome their troubles

____ 7. ARVIN G. Wants to marry Mama

____ 8. PATRONA H. Esperanza's new friend who helps watch the twins

____ 9. MELINA I. Pattern in Abuelita's blanket

____ 10. IMMIGRATION J. Mexican workers could use it on Friday afternoons.

____ 11. PINATA K. Esperanza's mother

____ 12. STRIKERS L. Esperanza's maternal grandmother

____ 13. POOL M. Spanish for "head of the household"

____ 14. ZIGZAG N. Cause the twins to become ill

____ 15. ORTEGA O. What Isabel wants for Christmas

____ 16. JOSEFINA P. Esperanza's job at the camp when she first arrives

____ 17. PLUMS Q. They hide dangerous "surprises" in the harvest.

____ 18. PHOENIX R. Gives Mama two hens for her future; the "egg lady"

____ 19. ANYTHING S. Boy Esperanza declared she would marry one day

____ 20. GRAPES T. Isabel's mother

II. Multiple Choice

1. Which statement best describes Abuelita?
   A. Abuelita is the housekeeper. She is an Indian from Oaxaco, with a short, solid figure and a braid down her back.
   B. Abuelita is Papa's mother. She is a stern woman of whom Esperanza is frightened. She runs the household and bosses everyone around.
   C. Abuelita is a taller, younger version of Mama. She is Mama's younger sister and she wears bright colored clothing and fancy diamond jewelry every day.
   D. Abuelita is a smaller, older, more wrinkled version of Mama. She looks very distinguished, wearing a respectable black dress, the same gold loops she wears in her ears every day, and her white hair pulled back into a bun at the nape of her neck.

2. What does Esperanza feed Lupe and Pepe that makes them sick?
   A. Plums
   B. Almonds
   C. Onions
   D. Cantaloupes

3. What item does Mama ask for that Esperanza takes out of her valise?
   A. Mama asks for a shawl to cover her shoulders.
   B. Mama asks for Abuelita's unfinished blanket.
   C. Mama asks for Esperanza's doll.
   D. Mama asks for Papa's belt with the silver buckle.

4. What is Esperanza's first job?
   A. Cutting potato eyes
   B. Sorting peaches
   C. Tying grape vines
   D. Packing asparagus

5. Which statement best describes the strikers' camp?
   A. The camp is brand new with running hot water, indoor toilets, and a pool.
   B. There are plenty of cabins for everyone and they have running water indoors.
   C. The camp is a little nicer than Esperanza's camp, but the strikers are paid less money.
   D. There are ten toilets for hundreds of people, people live in tents, the kitchens are outdoors, and children bathe in an irrigation ditch.

6. Why was a man with a gun riding on the truck with Esperanza and the other working women?
    A. He was on the truck to intimidate the women and scare them into working harder.
    B. He was on the truck to keep the women from striking.
    C. He was on the truck to protect the workers from the strikers.
    D. He was on the truck to keep the women from escaping.

7. How does Esperanza help Marta?
    A. Esperanza gives Marta an apron so she looks like one of the workers and won't be arrested by immigration.
    B. Esperanza gives Marta money to help her mother.
    C. Esperanza gives Marta food and shelter when she is kicked out of her camp.
    D. Esperanza helps Marta get a job at the farm.

8. Why does Miguel lose his job as a mechanic at the railroad?
    A. Miguel loses his job because a group of men from Oklahoma show up and offer to work for half the money.
    B. Miguel loses his job because he confronts his boss and asks for more money.
    C. Miguel loses his job because he is late for work one day and it makes his boss angry.
    D. Miguel quits his job because it doesn't pay well enough.

9. Why does Alfonso come to get Esperanza at the shed?
    A. Alfonso has found Esperanza's missing money orders.
    B. The twins are sick and he needs her to nurse them back to health.
    C. Mama's illness has returned and she has sent Alfonso to get Esperanza.
    D. Alfonso has received a message from Miguel asking him to bring Esperanza to the bus station at three o'clock.

10. What does Marta announce at the jamaica?
    A. She announces that Esperanza doesn't know how to sweep.
    B. She announces that she is selling a box full of kittens.
    C. She announces that the cotton workers will strike the following day.
    D. She announces her engagement to Miguel.

11. What are Esperanza's two jobs at the camp?
    A. She is responsible for cleaning the toilets and peeling onions.
    B. She is responsible for crocheting and mending clothes.
    C. She is responsible for taking care of the twins and sweeping the platform.
    D. She is responsible for picking onions and washing dishes.

12. Who are Tio Luis and Tio Marco? What do they bring to Mama the night Papa is late coming home?
    A. They are Papa's older stepbrothers. Tio Luis is the bank president and Tio Marco is the mayor of the town. They bring Mama the silver belt buckle that belongs to Papa.
    B. They are Esperanza's favorite uncles. They bring Mama some chocolates and flowers.
    C. They are Papa's best friends. They bring Mama gifts from the United States.
    D. They are campesinos who are unhappy working on the ranch. They bring Mama the silver belt buckle that belongs to Papa.

13. What does Senor Rodriguez bring to the ranch the day after Papa dies?
    A. He brings his daughter Marisol to comfort Esperanza.
    B. He brings the papayas that Papa had ordered for the fiesta.
    C. He brings a rosary for Esperanza so she can pray for her father.
    D. He brings Esperanza a doll - a present for her thirteenth birthday.

14. Why does Tio Luis want to marry Mama?
    A. He is in love with Mama and wants to take care of her in her time of need.
    B. Tio Luis loves Mama's house and wants to live in it. He has to marry her to do so.
    C. Tio Luis wants to enter politics, and he needs Mama's influence among the people to win an election. Mama is loved and respected by the people of the region.
    D. He wants to marry Mama so that Esperanza has a father figure in her life.

15. Who is responsible for setting fire to El Rancho de las Rosas?
    A. Bandits
    B. Campesinos
    C. Tio Luis and Tio Marco
    D. Miguel

16. Which statement best describes the train car in which Esperanza and Mama travel?
    A. The car is lined with tables covered in white linens and finely dressed servers are waiting to take lunch orders.
    B. The car is crowded with animals and hay is scattered all over the floor.
    C. The car is clean and spacious with plenty of room for the well-dressed travelers to sit comfortably.
    D. The car is crowded with peasants sitting on wooden benches and trash is scattered on the floor.

17. Why is Esperanza shocked that Mama is telling Carmen "the egg woman" about their troubles?
    A. Esperanza thinks Mama should not talk to strangers, especially since Tio Luis could have spies on the lookout.
    B. Esperanza thinks Mama is being mean to the woman and she's ashamed of Mama's behavior.
    C. Esperanza thinks the "egg woman" is ugly and Mama should only talk to beautiful women.
    D. Esperanza is shocked because when they lived in Aguascalientes Mama would have said it was inappropriate to tell "an egg woman" their problems.

18. Why does Esperanza become upset when the family stops for lunch on their way to the camp?
    A. Esperanza becomes upset because she can't hear the heartbeat of the valley.
    B. Esperanza and Miguel get into an argument.
    C. She misses her father.
    D. Mama becomes angry with Esperanza because of her bad attitude.

19. According to Marta, why don't the field owners mix workers of different ethnic groups?
    A. Marta claims that the owners don't want the workers banding together for higher wages or better housing.
    B. Marta claims the owners think the workers are more efficient when they are with other people from the same culture who speak the same language.
    C. Marta claims the owners are racist and don't want the Mexicans mixing with any other races.
    D. Marta doesn't know why the owners keep the workers from mixing.

20. A few days before Esperanza's birthday, she begs Miguel to drive her to the foothills before sunrise. Why?
    A. It is her tradition to visit the foothills on the morning of her birthday.
    B. She loves to see the sunrise there.
    C. She wants to lie down on the ground to listen to the earth's heartbeat.
    D. She wants to visit her father's grave.

III. Quotations: Explain the importance and meaning of the following quotations:

1. At first, they stayed only a few hours, but soon they became like la calabaza, the squash plant in Alfonso's garden, whose giant leaves spread out, encroaching upon anything smaller.

2. "I am poor, but I am rich. I have my children, I have a garden with roses, and I have my faith and the memories of those who have gone before me. What more is there?"

3. "Here, we have two choices. To be together and miserable or to be together and happy... I choose to be happy. So which will you choose?"

4. "Americans see us as one big brown group who are good for only manual labor."

5. Miguel had been right about never giving up, and she had been right, too, about rising above those who held them down.

IV. Composition
1. How are Esperanza and her family impacted by segregation and discrimination?

V. Vocabulary

____ 1. RESOUNDING A. Lacking in variety; boring

____ 2. SERENADED B. Looked at with wonder, admiration, or shock

____ 3. CORRUPT C. Entertained with a vocal or instrumental performance of music outdoors at night, esp. by a lover under the window of his sweetheart

____ 4. PENETRATE D. Pierce or pass into or through

____ 5. SALVAGE E. Not flowing or running, as water, air, etc.

____ 6. INDEBTED F. Causing serious mood

____ 7. VENOM G. Easily influenced; weak

____ 8. UNDULATING H. Having a wave-like or rippled form or surface

____ 9. MONOTONOUS I. Owing for favors or kindness received

____ 10. STAGNANT J. Guilty of dishonest practices; untrustworthy

____ 11. JALOPY K. Making an echoing sound

____ 12. SOLEMNLY L. Tightly drawn; tense

____ 13. EXTRAVAGANT M. Poison

____ 14. FRAYED N. Tending towards extreme or excessive spending

____ 15. YEARNING O. Falling apart automobile

____ 16. TAUT P. Worn away or tattered along the edges

____ 17. SUSCEPTIBLE Q. Leaning back

____ 18. RELUCTANTLY R. Unsatisfied desire

____ 19. MARVELED S. Unwillingly; disinclined

____ 20. RECLINING T. Saving something from fire, danger, etc.

Esperanza Rising Multiple Choice Unit Test 2 Answer Key

I. Matching

L	1.	ABUELITA	A.	Setting of the camp where Esperanza and Mama live and work in California
S	2.	MIGUEL	B.	Esperanza's last name
G	3.	LUIS	C.	Bought for Mama but given to the campesino family at the strikers' camp
R	4.	CARMEN	D.	la Migra; sent the strikers to Mexico
K	5.	RAMONA	E.	Main crop of El Rancho de las Rosas
P	6.	SWEEPING	F.	Metaphor Abuelita uses to describe how they will overcome their troubles
A	7.	ARVIN	G.	Wants to marry Mama
M	8.	PATRONA	H.	Esperanza's new friend who helps watch the twins
H	9.	MELINA	I.	Pattern in Abuelita's blanket
D	10.	IMMIGRATION	J.	Mexican workers could use it on Friday afternoons.
C	11.	PINATA	K.	Esperanza's mother
Q	12.	STRIKERS	L.	Esperanza's maternal grandmother
J	13.	POOL	M.	Spanish for "head of the household"
I	14.	ZIGZAG	N.	Cause the twins to become ill
B	15.	ORTEGA	O.	What Isabel wants for Christmas
T	16.	JOSEFINA	P.	Esperanza's job at the camp when she first arrives
N	17.	PLUMS	Q.	They hide dangerous "surprises" in the harvest.
F	18.	PHOENIX	R.	Gives Mama two hens for her future; the "egg lady"
O	19.	ANYTHING	S.	Boy Esperanza declared she would marry one day
E	20.	GRAPES	T.	Isabel's mother

II. Multiple Choice

D 1. Which statement best describes Abuelita?
   A. Abuelita is the housekeeper. She is an Indian from Oaxaco, with a short, solid figure and a braid down her back.
   B. Abuelita is Papa's mother. She is a stern woman of whom Esperanza is frightened. She runs the household and bosses everyone around.
   C. Abuelita is a taller, younger version of Mama. She is Mama's younger sister and she wears bright colored clothing and fancy diamond jewelry every day.
   D. Abuelita is a smaller, older, more wrinkled version of Mama. She looks very distinguished, wearing a respectable black dress, the same gold loops she wears in her ears every day, and her white hair pulled back into a bun at the nape of her neck.

A 2. What does Esperanza feed Lupe and Pepe that makes them sick?
   A. Plums
   B. Almonds
   C. Onions
   D. Cantaloupes

B 3. What item does Mama ask for that Esperanza takes out of her valise?
   A. Mama asks for a shawl to cover her shoulders.
   B. Mama asks for Abuelita's unfinished blanket.
   C. Mama asks for Esperanza's doll.
   D. Mama asks for Papa's belt with the silver buckle.

A 4. What is Esperanza's first job?
   A. Cutting potato eyes
   B. Sorting peaches
   C. Tying grape vines
   D. Packing asparagus

D 5. Which statement best describes the strikers' camp?
   A. The camp is brand new with running hot water, indoor toilets, and a pool.
   B. There are plenty of cabins for everyone and they have running water indoors.
   C. The camp is a little nicer than Esperanza's camp, but the strikers are paid less money.
   D. There are ten toilets for hundreds of people, people live in tents, the kitchens are outdoors, and children bathe in an irrigation ditch.

C 6. Why was a man with a gun riding on the truck with Esperanza and the other working women?
- A. He was on the truck to intimidate the women and scare them into working harder.
- B. He was on the truck to keep the women from striking.
- C. He was on the truck to protect the workers from the strikers.
- D. He was on the truck to keep the women from escaping.

A 7. How does Esperanza help Marta?
- A. Esperanza gives Marta an apron so she looks like one of the workers and won't be arrested by immigration.
- B. Esperanza gives Marta money to help her mother.
- C. Esperanza gives Marta food and shelter when she is kicked out of her camp.
- D. Esperanza helps Marta get a job at the farm.

A 8. Why does Miguel lose his job as a mechanic at the railroad?
- A. Miguel loses his job because a group of men from Oklahoma show up and offer to work for half the money.
- B. Miguel loses his job because he confronts his boss and asks for more money.
- C. Miguel loses his job because he is late for work one day and it makes his boss angry.
- D. Miguel quits his job because it doesn't pay well enough.

D 9. Why does Alfonso come to get Esperanza at the shed?
- A. Alfonso has found Esperanza's missing money orders.
- B. The twins are sick and he needs her to nurse them back to health.
- C. Mama's illness has returned and she has sent Alfonso to get Esperanza.
- D. Alfonso has received a message from Miguel asking him to bring Esperanza to the bus station at three o'clock.

C 10. What does Marta announce at the jamaica?
- A. She announces that Esperanza doesn't know how to sweep.
- B. She announces that she is selling a box full of kittens.
- C. She announces that the cotton workers will strike the following day.
- D. She announces her engagement to Miguel.

C 11. What are Esperanza's two jobs at the camp?
- A. She is responsible for cleaning the toilets and peeling onions.
- B. She is responsible for crocheting and mending clothes.
- C. She is responsible for taking care of the twins and sweeping the platform.
- D. She is responsible for picking onions and washing dishes.

A 12. Who are Tio Luis and Tio Marco? What do they bring to Mama the night Papa is late coming home?
   A. They are Papa's older stepbrothers. Tio Luis is the bank president and Tio Marco is the mayor of the town. They bring Mama the silver belt buckle that belongs to Papa.
   B. They are Esperanza's favorite uncles. They bring Mama some chocolates and flowers.
   C. They are Papa's best friends. They bring Mama gifts from the United States.
   D. They are campesinos who are unhappy working on the ranch. They bring Mama the silver belt buckle that belongs to Papa.

B 13. What does Senor Rodriguez bring to the ranch the day after Papa dies?
   A. He brings his daughter Marisol to comfort Esperanza.
   B. He brings the papayas that Papa had ordered for the fiesta.
   C. He brings a rosary for Esperanza so she can pray for her father.
   D. He brings Esperanza a doll - a present for her thirteenth birthday.

C 14. Why does Tio Luis want to marry Mama?
   A. He is in love with Mama and wants to take care of her in her time of need.
   B. Tio Luis loves Mama's house and wants to live in it. He has to marry her to do so.
   C. Tio Luis wants to enter politics, and he needs Mama's influence among the people to win an election. Mama is loved and respected by the people of the region.
   D. He wants to marry Mama so that Esperanza has a father figure in her life.

C 15. Who is responsible for setting fire to El Rancho de las Rosas?
   A. Bandits
   B. Campesinos
   C. Tio Luis and Tio Marco
   D. Miguel

D 16. Which statement best describes the train car in which Esperanza and Mama travel?
   A. The car is lined with tables covered in white linens and finely dressed servers are waiting to take lunch orders.
   B. The car is crowded with animals and hay is scattered all over the floor.
   C. The car is clean and spacious with plenty of room for the well-dressed travelers to sit comfortably.
   D. The car is crowded with peasants sitting on wooden benches and trash is scattered on the floor.

D 17. Why is Esperanza shocked that Mama is telling Carmen "the egg woman" about their troubles?
   A. Esperanza thinks Mama should not talk to strangers, especially since Tio Luis could have spies on the lookout.
   B. Esperanza thinks Mama is being mean to the woman and she's ashamed of Mama's behavior.
   C. Esperanza thinks the "egg woman" is ugly and Mama should only talk to beautiful women.
   D. Esperanza is shocked because when they lived in Aguascalientes Mama would have said it was inappropriate to tell "an egg woman" their problems.

A 18. Why does Esperanza become upset when the family stops for lunch on their way to the camp?
   A. Esperanza becomes upset because she can't hear the heartbeat of the valley.
   B. Esperanza and Miguel get into an argument.
   C. She misses her father.
   D. Mama becomes angry with Esperanza because of her bad attitude.

A 19. According to Marta, why don't the field owners mix workers of different ethnic groups?
   A. Marta claims that the owners don't want the workers banding together for higher wages or better housing.
   B. Marta claims the owners think the workers are more efficient when they are with other people from the same culture who speak the same language.
   C. Marta claims the owners are racist and don't want the Mexicans mixing with any other races.
   D. Marta doesn't know why the owners keep the workers from mixing.

C 20. A few days before Esperanza's birthday, she begs Miguel to drive her to the foothills before sunrise. Why?
   A. It is her tradition to visit the foothills on the morning of her birthday.
   B. She loves to see the sunrise there.
   C. She wants to lie down on the ground to listen to the earth's heartbeat.
   D. She wants to visit her father's grave.

V. Vocabulary

K	1.	RESOUNDING	A.	Lacking in variety; boring
C	2.	SERENADED	B.	Looked at with wonder, admiration, or shock
J	3.	CORRUPT	C.	Entertained with a vocal or instrumental performance of music outdoors at night, esp. by a lover under the window of his sweetheart
D	4.	PENETRATE	D.	Pierce or pass into or through
T	5.	SALVAGE	E.	Not flowing or running, as water, air, etc.
I	6.	INDEBTED	F.	Causing serious mood
M	7.	VENOM	G.	Easily influenced; weak
H	8.	UNDULATING	H.	Having a wave-like or rippled form or surface
A	9.	MONOTONOUS	I.	Owing for favors or kindness received
E	10.	STAGNANT	J.	Guilty of dishonest practices; untrustworthy
O	11.	JALOPY	K.	Making an echoing sound
F	12.	SOLEMNLY	L.	Tightly drawn; tense
N	13.	EXTRAVAGANT	M.	Poison
P	14.	FRAYED	N.	Tending towards extreme or excessive spending
R	15.	YEARNING	O.	Falling apart automobile
L	16.	TAUT	P.	Worn away or tattered along the edges
G	17.	SUSCEPTIBLE	Q.	Leaning back
S	18.	RELUCTANTLY	R.	Unsatisfied desire
B	19.	MARVELED	S.	Unwillingly; disinclined
Q	20.	RECLINING	T.	Saving something from fire, danger, etc.

Esperanza Rising Advanced Short Answer Unit Test

I. Matching

____ 1. ABUELITA   A. Wants to be the Queen of May

____ 2. HORTENSIA   B. Hortensia is from there.

____ 3. QUINCEANERA   C. Isabel's father

____ 4. LUIS   D. Promised Miguel he would help him get a job on the railroad one day

____ 5. DOLL   E. Lupe and Pepe

____ 6. PAPA   F. Papa's last gift to Esperanza

____ 7. ISABEL   G. Esperanza's maternal grandmother

____ 8. TWINS   H. la Migra; sent the strikers to Mexico

____ 9. FLAN   I. Mayor of Aguascalientes

____ 10. JUAN   J. Field-workers

____ 11. ADA   K. A presentation party that girls have when they turn fifteen in Mexico

____ 12. IMMIGRATION   L. Wants to marry Mama

____ 13. EYES   M. Metaphor Abuelita uses to describe how they will overcome their troubles

____ 14. GROTTO   N. Marta's mother

____ 15. MARCO   O. Esperanza's father

____ 16. SIXTO   P. Made by Josefina to sell at the jamaica

____ 17. NUNS   Q. Contains a statue of Our Lady of Guadalupe

____ 18. PHOENIX   R. Esperanza has to cut these off the potatoes

____ 19. CAMPESINOS   S. Esperanza's housekeeper

____ 20. OAXACA   T. Abuelita's sisters who help Mama and Esperanza get their traveling papers

II. Short Answer
1. What does the scene in which Esperanza and her father lie down to hear the heartbeat of the earth reveal about their relationship?

2. What does the story of Miguel, the mouse, and the house thieves reveal about his character?

3. Describe Esperanza's first encounter with Marta. What does the encounter reveal about Marta's character? What does it reveal about Esperanza's character?

4. What does Esperanza mean when she says to Miguel that there is a "deep river" that runs between them?

5. Compare Papa to Tio Luis and Tio Marco.

6. Compare Mama's and Esperanza's reactions to their new lives. Who would you most resemble if you were in the same situation?

7. When the women are taking a bath, Esperanza runs to get hot water for Hortensia before anyone else could. Why does she do this? What does it show about her transformation?

8. Compare the strikers' camp to the camp in which Esperanza lives. How is Esperanza affected by the strikers' camp? Did reading about the camp affect you? How?

9. How is Esperanza's life different at the camp than in Mexico?

10. Esperanza and Miguel see Esperanza's pinata hanging from a tree in the strikers' camp. What does the pinata symbolize?

III. Quotations: Explain the importance and meaning of the following quotations:

1. "The rich take care of the rich and the poor take care of those who have less than they have."

2. "Here, we have two choices. To be together and miserable or to be together and happy... I choose to be happy. So which will you choose?"

3. The mountains and valleys in the blanket were easy. But as soon as she reached a mountain, she was headed back down into a valley again. Would she ever escape this valley she was living in?

4. The strikers only listened if you agreed with them.

5. When Esperanza told Abuelita their story, about all that had happened to them, she didn't measure time by the usual seasons. Instead, she told it as a field-worker, in spans of fruits and vegetables and by what needed to be done to the land.

IV. Composition
1. How does Esperanza change throughout the story and how does her development reflect the author's main themes?

V. Vocabulary
   A. Write the vocabulary words you are given. After writing them down, go back and write in their definitions.

Word	Definition
1	
2	
3	
4	
5	
6	
7	
8	
9	
10	

   B. Write a paragraph about the book using 8 of the 10 vocabulary words above.

Esperanza Rising Advanced Short Answer Unit Test Answer Key

I. Matching

G	1.	ABUELITA	A.	Wants to be the Queen of May
S	2.	HORTENSIA	B.	Hortensia is from there.
K	3.	QUINCEANERA	C.	Isabel's father
L	4.	LUIS	D.	Promised Miguel he would help him get a job on the railroad one day
F	5.	DOLL	E.	Lupe and Pepe
D	6.	PAPA	F.	Papa's last gift to Esperanza
A	7.	ISABEL	G.	Esperanza's maternal grandmother
E	8.	TWINS	H.	la Migra; sent the strikers to Mexico
P	9.	FLAN	I.	Mayor of Aguascalientes
C	10.	JUAN	J.	Field-workers
N	11.	ADA	K.	A presentation party that girls have when they turn fifteen in Mexico
H	12.	IMMIGRATION	L.	Wants to marry Mama
R	13.	EYES	M.	Metaphor Abuelita uses to describe how they will overcome their troubles
Q	14.	GROTTO	N.	Marta's mother
I	15.	MARCO	O.	Esperanza's father
O	16.	SIXTO	P.	Made by Josefina to sell at the jamaica
T	17.	NUNS	Q.	Contains a statue of Our Lady of Guadalupe
M	18.	PHOENIX	R.	Esperanza has to cut these off the potatoes
J	19.	CAMPESINOS	S.	Esperanza's housekeeper
B	20.	OAXACA	T.	Abuelita's sisters who help Mama and Esperanza get their traveling papers

V. Vocabulary

　　Write the vocabulary words and definitions you will use for this test.

Word	Definition
1	
2	
3	
4	
5	
6	
7	
8	
9	
10	

Select the vocabulary words for the Advanced Short Answer Test

UNIT RESOURCE MATERIALS

BULLETIN BOARD IDEAS *Esperanza Rising*

1. Save one corner of the board for the best samples of students' *Esperanza Rising* writing assignments.
2. Take one of the word search puzzles from the extra activities packet and with a marker copy it over in a larger size on the bulletin board. Write the clues on one side. Invite students prior to and after class to find the words and circle them on the bulletin board.
3. Write several of the most significant quotations from the book onto the board. Invite students to write their reflections about the quotations directly onto the bulletin board. Make sure to clarify what is and isn't appropriate language for a public bulletin board.
4. Make a word wall using the vocabulary from this unit. As you complete sections of the novel and discuss the vocabulary for each section, write the definitions on the bulletin board. (If your board is one students face frequently, it will help them learn the words.)
5. Each day, have students predict what is going to happen in the next reading assignment and post the prediction on the board. Make sure to review the predictions after the assignment has been read and discussed in class.
6. Have students create maps of El Rancho de las Rosas and the Arvin Camp. Encourage students to use color and label important items on the maps. You may want to have them include quotations describing the setting.
7. Have students draw a portrait of one of the characters and write a short description or poem to accompany the picture.
8. Post pictures and articles about the Great Depression. You may want to highlight the effects of the Great Depression on settings mentioned in *Esperanza Rising* like California, Oklahoma, and Texas. You may also want to emphasize the effects it had on the jobs mentioned in the book as well (like farm labor and railroad workers).
9. How much do students know about the Mexican Revolution? Create a bulletin board packed with pictures and articles about the revolution. Consider highlighting the Aguascalientes region. It would be fascinating to compare a peasant's story with that of a landowner.
10. Post a map showing the route that Esperanza took to get from Aguascalientes, Mexico to Arvin California.
11. Split the bulletin board in half. On one side, post pictures of the Mexican culture of the 1930s. What clothing was in style? What were some popular dishes? What was the caste system and society like? On the other side of the board, post pictures displaying the same information for 1930s California.

RELATED TOPICS *Esperanza Rising*

1. Farming/Agriculture
2. Children and the Great Depression
3. Migrant Camps
4. Farm Workers' Union
5. Cesar E. Chavez
6. Mexican Recipes
7. Mexican Birthday Traditions
8. Mexican Proverbs
9. Pneumonia
10. The San Joaquin Valley
11. Growing Roses
12. Crocheting
13. The Dust Bowl
14. California's Agricultural History
15. Valley Fever
16. Migrant Workers
17. Immigration
18. Mexico
19. The Mexican Revolution
20. The Great Depression
21. Oaxaca, Mexico
22. Zapotec Indians
23. Post-revolutionary Mexico
24. Mexican Caste System
25. 1930s Railroads
26. Oklahoma and the Great Depression
27. Travel by Train

MORE ACTIVITIES *Esperanza Rising*

1. Watch *Riding the Rails*, a documentary about 250,000 teenagers who rode freight trains across the country during the Great Depression. Have students compare and contrast Esperanza's experience with that of the rail riding teens.

2. Have students research various labor strikes that have happened in history. Some of the more noteworthy ones are: Homstead Strike (1892), Pullman Strike (1893), Ludlow Massacre (1914), Postal Workers' Strike (1970), Air Traffic Controllers' Strike (1981), UPS Workers (1997), Screen Actors Guild (2000), NYC Transit Workers (2005), Writers' Guild (1988). Students should research and report on the causes and effects of the strikes.

3. Have students research about the Great Depression. As a class, brainstorm a list of bad things that happened because of the Depression--and then make a list of good things that came from it. (After all, Esperanza is about hope!)

4. Immigration is as American as apple pie. Have students research about periods of time when large groups of people have come to America. Compare and contrast the things that caused them to come, how each group did (or did not) assimilate into the American culture, and the response of the American people to each group.

5. Migrant workers and immigrants often need help when they come to America. Do a class fundraising project and donate the proceeds to a needy family in your school's neighborhood.

6. Have students work together to make a time line of the events in the story. Tape a large piece of butcher paper to one wall and have students write in the events directly onto the paper. Students may want to add drawings or cut-out pictures to represent the events.

7. Have students write a diary that one of the story's main characters might have kept before, during, or after the book's events. Remind students that the character's thoughts and feelings are very important in a diary. Consider allowing students to add illustrations to their diaries.

8. Have students interview a character from *Esperanza Rising*. Students should write at least ten questions that will give the character the opportunity to discuss his/her thoughts and feelings about his/her role in the story. Consider choosing the best interviews to be presented to the class in a dramatic fashion. One student could act the part of the interviewer and another student could play the role of the character.

9. Food plays an important role in the book. Divide the class into groups. Assign each group one of the fruits or vegetables mentioned in the book (just refer to the chapter titles). Have each group bring in a dish featuring their assigned produce. They may want to refer to the text to see what dishes were prepared in the book using the same products (like the papaya salad Esperanza loves or flan de almendra).

10. Crocheting is not only a past-time for Esperanza, but it is also an important activity in the book. Have students learn to crochet. There are many websites dedicated to the art of crochet. One example is: http://learntocrochet.lionbrand.com. Alternatively, invite a knowledgeable parent or grandparent to come in and teach the class.

11. Many students have never actually seen where the country's food is grown or met the people responsible for keeping our grocery stores stocked. Take students on a field trip to a farm, an orchard, or a vineyard. If a field trip is not possible, bring in a guest speaker such as a farmer or a field laborer.

12. Host a jamaica. Have students brainstorm the activities and types of food they would like to have at the jamaica. Then, break the class into committees and have each group responsible for one element of the jamaica. Some categories may include entertainment, food, and decorations. At the camp's jamaica, the women were selling food. You could even make this into a fundraiser and invite the whole school to your jamaica.

13. When Esperanza and Mama moved to California, they were only able to pack a few items to take with them. Pose the following question to students: "If you had to leave your home forever and were only allowed to bring one suitcase, what would you pack?" Then, have students do one of the following: Students can draw an imaginary suitcase and then fill it with words or symbols representing the things they would take. Or, students can literally fill a suitcase with the items they would take and bring it to school for show-and-tell. You may want to have students write a paragraph or two explaining why they chose these items.

14. At the end of the novel, Esperanza feels like she is soaring above the valley. Take your students to Google Earth (http://earth.google.com) and look at your own neighborhood from above. (You will need to download the software, so be sure to do this prior to class time.) You could also have students look at Arvin, California or Aguascalientes, Mexico to help deepen their understanding of the setting.

15. Host a literary tea party. There are two variations to this post-reading activity. In method one, the teacher tapes the name of a character to the back of each student. The student does not know the name of his character and must guess who he is based upon the conversations he has with other students. He may ask any question except for "What is my name?". In method two, the teacher gives each student a card with a character's name. The students do not share the name of their characters with one another. Each student becomes the character on his card and mingles with the other students. Classmates will then guess which character each student has become. You may want to bring in punch and cookies to add some fun to the party.

16. Create a biographical poem about any character by following the format below:

    Line 1: Character's first name
    Line 2: Who is...(Descriptive words that describe the character)
    Line 3: Who is related to...
    Line 4: Who loves...(three ideas or people)
    Line 5: Who feels...(three ideas)
    Line 6: Who needs...(three ideas)
    Line 7: Who gives...(three ideas)
    Line 8: Who fears...(three ideas)
    Line 9: Who would like to see...
    Line 10: Who shares...
    Line 11: Who is a resident of...
    Line 12: Character's last name

17. Have students design a bulletin board (ready to be put up) for *Esperanza Rising*.

18. Have students design a book cover (front, back, and inside flaps) for *Esperanza Rising*. Consider using a manila folder for this activity because students can use it to store their pre-reading vocabulary worksheets and study guide questions. Encourage students to also keep any other worksheets, drawings, or compositions that they generate in the folder. It's nice to have everything in one place!

19. Have students choose one chapter of the book to rewrite as a play. You can have students perform the skit in front of the class or film it at home. Encourage students to wear costumes and incorporate props.

20. Have students write a letter to a movie producer in which they pitch the idea of making *Esperanza Rising* into a movie. Students should explain why the story, characters, conflicts, etc., would make a good film. They should suggest a filming location and the actors to play the various roles. Then, have students create a movie poster to accompany the letter. Consider displaying the letters and movie posters on the bulletin board.

UNIT WORD LIST *Esperanza Rising*

No.	Word	Clue/Definition
1.	ABUELITA	Esperanza's maternal grandmother
2.	ADA	Marta's mother
3.	AGUASCALIENTES	Location of El Rancho de las Rosas
4.	ALFONSO	Hortensia's husband and Miguel's father
5.	ANYTHING	What Isabel wants for Christmas
6.	ARVIN	Setting of the camp where Esperanza and Mama live and work in California
7.	AVOCADO	Esperanza puts this on her hands to make them soft again
8.	BLANKET	Given to Esperanza by Abuelita with the instructions to finish it while waiting for Abuelita to join them in California
9.	CAMPESINOS	Field-workers
10.	CARMEN	Gives Mama two hens for her future; the "egg lady"
11.	DOLL	Papa's last gift to Esperanza
12.	EYES	Esperanza has to cut these off the potatoes
13.	FIESTA	Celebrates the end of the harvest and Esperanza's birthday
14.	FIRE	Destroys the Ortegas' house
15.	FLAN	Made by Josefina to sell at the jamaica
16.	GRAPES	Main crop of El Rancho de las Rosas
17.	GROTTO	Contains a statue of Our Lady of Guadalupe
18.	HORTENSIA	Esperanza's housekeeper
19.	IMMIGRATION	La Migra; sent the strikers to Mexico
20.	ISABEL	Wants to be the Queen of May
21.	JAMAICAS	Summer camp parties with music and food held every Saturday night
22.	JOSEFINA	Isabel's mother
23.	JUAN	Isabel's father
24.	LAND	Esperanza can feel its heart beating.
25.	LUIS	Wants to marry Mama
26.	MARCO	Mayor of Aguascalientes
27.	MARISOL	Esperanza's best friend
28.	MARTA	Wants the workers to band together and strike
29.	MELINA	Esperanza's new friend who helps watch the twins
30.	MIGUEL	Boy Esperanza declared she would marry one day
31.	NUNS	Abuelita's sisters who help Mama and Esperanza get their traveling papers
32.	OAXACA	Hortensia is from there.
33.	ORTEGA	Esperanza's last name
34.	PAPA	Promised Miguel he would help him get a job on the railroad one day
35.	PATRONA	Spanish for "head of the household"

No.	Word	Clue/Definition
36.	PHOENIX	Metaphor Abuelita uses to describe how they will overcome their troubles
37.	PINATA	Bought for Mama but given to the campesino family at the strikers' camp
38.	PLUMS	Cause the twins to become ill
39.	POOL	Mexican workers could use it on Friday afternoons.
40.	QUINCEANERA	A presentation party that girls have when they turn fifteen in Mexico
41.	RAILROAD	Working there is Miguel's dream job.
42.	RAMONA	Esperanza's mother
43.	REINA	Miguel's nickname for Esperanza
44.	ROSES	Brought to California by Miguel and Alfonso as a surprise for Mama and Esperanza
45.	RYAN	Author of *Esperanza Rising*
46.	SIXTO	Esperanza's father
47.	STRIKERS	They hide dangerous "surprises" in the harvest.
48.	SWEEPING	Esperanza's job at the camp when she first arrives
49.	THORN	Makes Esperanza think, "bad luck"
50.	TWINS	Lupe and Pepe
51.	YAKOTA	Market owner who is kind to Mexicans
52.	ZIGZAG	Pattern in Abuelita's blanket

WORD SEARCH - Esperanza Rising

```
C A M P E S I N O S G R O T T O Y S A L
R T R O I W N Y C M N R B M K D A T B F
A R A O B N G M R U I F K M M A K R U V
I A M L M S A M A L H A B J P C O I E Y
L M O K V I V T M P T N S I A O T K L C
R C N S H X S X A L Y I X R S V A E I K
O O A C N T L A D A N F M F L A N R T M
A V S Y Q O C H O N A E H Z N J B S A N
D J G E S N R H A D N S O B F N F E A X
D J A I S P K H X L C O R R T S R L G
H W R M R T A P A K F J T V E X V H N K
P A N D A W Z P C Q C O E K I I L A G V
M D I M M I G R A T I O N U N S Y N D F
E L J X G N C N T N A A S S A R I R O Z
L E U Z F S O A Y T L Z I M O P G O L H
I U A J Z R X P S B G R A P E S F H L B
N G N H T G K E I C G X S E R Y H T R H
A I Y A P T I B U C F K W W I M E P Y T
D M P N B F B C L X R S B D F T Z S B H
```

ABUELITA	FIRE	MARCO	RAILROAD
ADA	FLAN	MARISOL	RAMONA
ALFONSO	GRAPES	MARTA	REINA
ANYTHING	GROTTO	MELINA	ROSES
ARVIN	HORTENSIA	MIGUEL	RYAN
AVOCADO	IMMIGRATION	NUNS	SIXTO
BLANKET	ISABEL	OAXACA	STRIKERS
CAMPESINOS	JAMAICAS	PAPA	SWEEPING
CARMEN	JOSEFINA	PATRONA	THORN
DOLL	JUAN	PINATA	TWINS
EYES	LAND	PLUMS	YAKOTA
FIESTA	LUIS	POOL	ZIGZAG

WORD SEARCH ANSWER KEY - Esperanza Rising

ABUELITA	FIRE	MARCO	RAILROAD
ADA	FLAN	MARISOL	RAMONA
ALFONSO	GRAPES	MARTA	REINA
ANYTHING	GROTTO	MELINA	ROSES
ARVIN	HORTENSIA	MIGUEL	RYAN
AVOCADO	IMMIGRATION	NUNS	SIXTO
BLANKET	ISABEL	OAXACA	STRIKERS
CAMPESINOS	JAMAICAS	PAPA	SWEEPING
CARMEN	JOSEFINA	PATRONA	THORN
DOLL	JUAN	PINATA	TWINS
EYES	LAND	PLUMS	YAKOTA
FIESTA	LUIS	POOL	ZIGZAG

CROSSWORD - Esperanza Rising

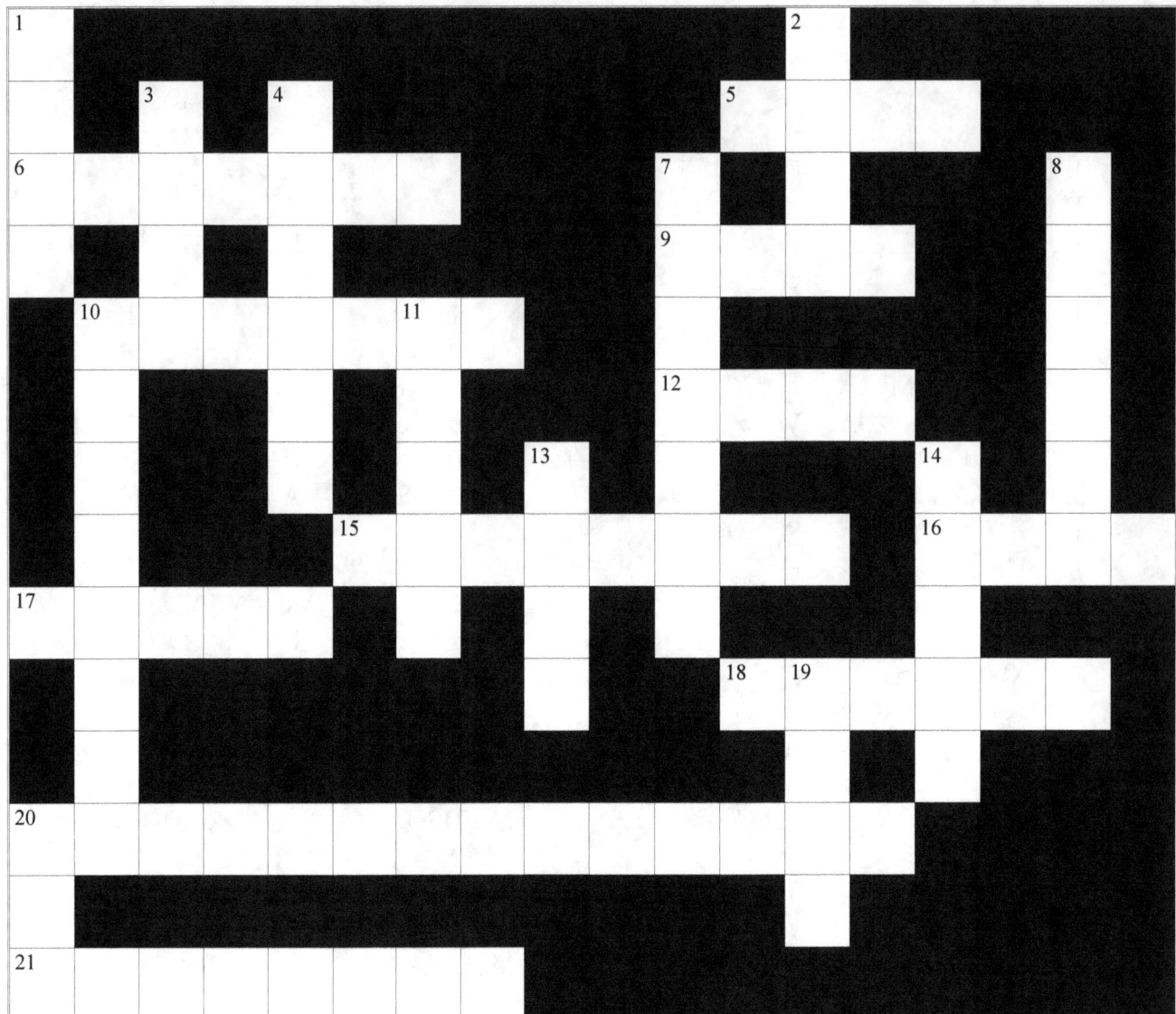

Across
- 5. Wants to marry Mama
- 6. Esperanza puts this on her hands to make them soft
- 9. Esperanza can feel its heart beating.
- 10. Hortensia's husband; Miguel's father
- 12. Abuelita's sisters who help Mama & Esperanza get their traveling papers
- 15. They hide dangerous surprises in the harvest.
- 16. Author of Esperanza Rising
- 17. Makes Esperanza think, 'Bad luck.'
- 18. Esperanza's new friend who helps watch the twins
- 20. Location of El Rancho de las Rosas
- 21. Esperanza's maternal grandmother

Down
- 1. Made by Josefina to sell at the jamaica
- 2. Isabel's father
- 3. Papa's last gift to Esperanza
- 4. Esperanza's mother
- 7. Esperanza has instructions to finish this while waiting for Abuelita
- 8. Celebrates the end of harvest & Esperanza's birthday
- 10. What Isabel wants for Christmas
- 11. Esperanza's father
- 13. Destroys the Ortegas' house
- 14. Location of the camp where Esperanza and Mama live and work in California
- 19. Esperanza cuts these off the potatoes
- 20. Marta's mother

CROSSWORD ANSWER KEY - Esperanza Rising

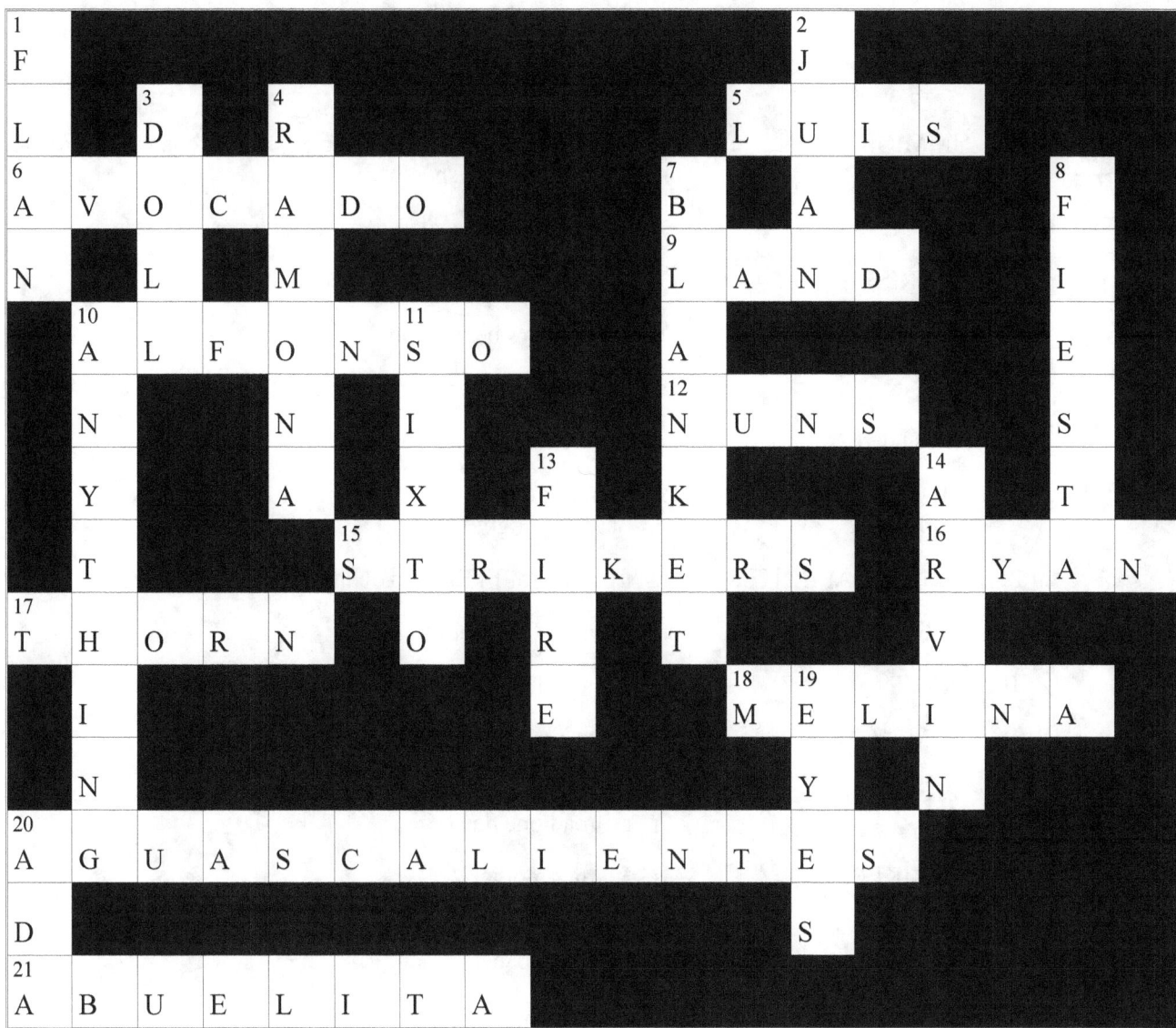

Across
- 5. Wants to marry Mama
- 6. Esperanza puts this on her hands to make them soft
- 9. Esperanza can feel its heart beating.
- 10. Hortensia's husband; Miguel's father
- 12. Abuelita's sisters who help Mama & Esperanza get their traveling papers
- 15. They hide dangerous surprises in the harvest.
- 16. Author of Esperanza Rising
- 17. Makes Esperanza think, 'Bad luck.'
- 18. Esperanza's new friend who helps watch the twins
- 20. Location of El Rancho de las Rosas
- 21. Esperanza's maternal grandmother

Down
- 1. Made by Josefina to sell at the jamaica
- 2. Isabel's father
- 3. Papa's last gift to Esperanza
- 4. Esperanza's mother
- 7. Esperanza has instructions to finish this while waiting for Abuelita
- 8. Celebrates the end of harvest & Esperanza's birthday
- 10. What Isabel wants for Christmas
- 11. Esperanza's father
- 13. Destroys the Ortegas' house
- 14. Location of the camp where Esperanza and Mama live and work in California
- 19. Esperanza cuts these off the potatoes
- 20. Marta's mother

MATCHING 1 *Esperanza Rising*

____ 1. IMMIGRATION   A. Brought to California by Miguel and Alfonso as a surprise for Mama and Esperanza

____ 2. PAPA   B. Boy Esperanza declared she would marry one day

____ 3. MARISOL   C. They hide dangerous "surprises" in the harvest.

____ 4. LUIS   D. Esperanza's best friend

____ 5. NUNS   E. Esperanza puts this on her hands to make them soft again

____ 6. MIGUEL   F. Esperanza's housekeeper

____ 7. HORTENSIA   G. Summer camp parties with music and food held every Saturday night

____ 8. AGUASCALIENTES   H. Location of El Rancho de las Rosas

____ 9. ORTEGA   I. Wants to marry Mama

____ 10. ARVIN   J. What Isabel wants for Christmas

____ 11. JAMAICAS   K. La Migra; sent the strikers to Mexico

____ 12. ZIGZAG   L. Promised Miguel he would help him get a job on the railroad one day

____ 13. STRIKERS   M. Marta's mother

____ 14. ADA   N. Abuelita's sisters who help Mama and Esperanza get their traveling papers

____ 15. AVOCADO   O. Esperanza's father

____ 16. ANYTHING   P. Setting of the camp where Esperanza and Mama live and work in California

____ 17. ROSES   Q. Esperanza's job at the camp when she first arrives

____ 18. SWEEPING   R. Pattern in Abuelita's blanket

____ 19. JUAN   S. Isabel's father

____ 20. SIXTO   T. Esperanza's last name

MATCHING 1 ANSWER KEY *Esperanza Rising*

K	1.	IMMIGRATION	A.	Brought to California by Miguel and Alfonso as a surprise for Mama and Esperanza
L	2.	PAPA	B.	Boy Esperanza declared she would marry one day
D	3.	MARISOL	C.	They hide dangerous "surprises" in the harvest.
I	4.	LUIS	D.	Esperanza's best friend
N	5.	NUNS	E.	Esperanza puts this on her hands to make them soft again
B	6.	MIGUEL	F.	Esperanza's housekeeper
F	7.	HORTENSIA	G.	Summer camp parties with music and food held every Saturday night
H	8.	AGUASCALIENTES	H.	Location of El Rancho de las Rosas
T	9.	ORTEGA	I.	Wants to marry Mama
P	10.	ARVIN	J.	What Isabel wants for Christmas
G	11.	JAMAICAS	K.	La Migra; sent the strikers to Mexico
R	12.	ZIGZAG	L.	Promised Miguel he would help him get a job on the railroad one day
C	13.	STRIKERS	M.	Marta's mother
M	14.	ADA	N.	Abuelita's sisters who help Mama and Esperanza get their traveling papers
E	15.	AVOCADO	O.	Esperanza's father
J	16.	ANYTHING	P.	Setting of the camp where Esperanza and Mama live and work in California
A	17.	ROSES	Q.	Esperanza's job at the camp when she first arrives
Q	18.	SWEEPING	R.	Pattern in Abuelita's blanket
S	19.	JUAN	S.	Isabel's father
O	20.	SIXTO	T.	Esperanza's last name

MATCHING 2 *Esperanza Rising*

____ 1. ISABEL   A. Cause the twins to become ill

____ 2. BLANKET   B. Esperanza's maternal grandmother

____ 3. PHOENIX   C. Bought for Mama but given to the campesino family at the strikers' camp

____ 4. QUINCEANERA D. Metaphor Abuelita uses to describe how they will overcome their troubles

____ 5. ALFONSO   E. A presentation party that girls have when they turn fifteen in Mexico

____ 6. ABUELITA   F. Mayor of Aguascalientes

____ 7. MARCO   G. Wants the workers to band together and strike

____ 8. CAMPESINOS H. Papa's last gift to Esperanza

____ 9. RAMONA   I. Hortensia's husband and Miguel's father

____ 10. DOLL   J. Wants to be the Queen of May

____ 11. CARMEN   K. Field-workers

____ 12. YAKOTA   L. Contains a statue of Our Lady of Guadalupe

____ 13. PINATA   M. Esperanza's mother

____ 14. MELINA   N. Miguel's nickname for Esperanza

____ 15. PLUMS   O. Given to Esperanza by Abuelita with the instructions to finish it while waiting for Abuelita to join them in California

____ 16. GROTTO   P. Esperanza's new friend who helps watch the twins

____ 17. MARTA   Q. Working there is Miguel's dream job.

____ 18. JOSEFINA   R. Market owner who is kind to Mexicans

____ 19. RAILROAD   S. Isabel's mother

____ 20. REINA   T. Gives Mama two hens for her future; the "egg lady"

MATCHING 2 ANSWER KEY *Esperanza Rising*

J	1.	ISABEL	A.	Cause the twins to become ill
O	2.	BLANKET	B.	Esperanza's maternal grandmother
D	3.	PHOENIX	C.	Bought for Mama but given to the campesino family at the strikers' camp
E	4.	QUINCEANERA	D.	Metaphor Abuelita uses to describe how they will overcome their troubles
I	5.	ALFONSO	E.	A presentation party that girls have when they turn fifteen in Mexico
B	6.	ABUELITA	F.	Mayor of Aguascalientes
F	7.	MARCO	G.	Wants the workers to band together and strike
K	8.	CAMPESINOS	H.	Papa's last gift to Esperanza
M	9.	RAMONA	I.	Hortensia's husband and Miguel's father
H	10.	DOLL	J.	Wants to be the Queen of May
T	11.	CARMEN	K.	Field-workers
R	12.	YAKOTA	L.	Contains a statue of Our Lady of Guadalupe
C	13.	PINATA	M.	Esperanza's mother
P	14.	MELINA	N.	Miguel's nickname for Esperanza
A	15.	PLUMS	O.	Given to Esperanza by Abuelita with the instructions to finish it while waiting for Abuelita to join them in California
L	16.	GROTTO	P.	Esperanza's new friend who helps watch the twins
G	17.	MARTA	Q.	Working there is Miguel's dream job.
S	18.	JOSEFINA	R.	Market owner who is kind to Mexicans
Q	19.	RAILROAD	S.	Isabel's mother
N	20.	REINA	T.	Gives Mama two hens for her future; the "egg lady"

JUGGLE 1 *Esperanza Rising*

_____ = 1. VRAIN
Setting of the camp where Esperanza and Mama live and work in California

_____ = 2. TELUAIAB
Esperanza's maternal grandmother

_____ = 3. USCELSATEAINAG
Location of El Rancho de las Rosas

_____ = 4. RCMOA
Mayor of Aguascalientes

_____ = 5. ERTGAO
Esperanza's last name

_____ = 6. MCEPISSONA
Field-workers

_____ = 7. OTXIS
Esperanza's father

_____ = 8. NAAMOR
Esperanza's mother

_____ = 9. PANOART
Spanish for "head of the household"

_____ = 10. OHRTEANSI
Esperanza's housekeeper

_____ = 11. SAOFLON
Hortensia's husband and Miguel's father

_____ = 12. RILAOARD
Working there is Miguel's dream job.

_____ = 13. ACRNME
Gives Mama two hens for her future; the "egg lady"

_____ = 14. ILMORAS
Esperanza's best friend

_____ = 15. SLIU
Wants to marry Mama

_____ = 16. SNNU
Abuelita's sisters who help Mama and Esperanza get their traveling papers

_____ = 17. PHNIEXO
Metaphor Abuelita uses to describe how they will overcome their troubles

_____ = 18. AANCREUINEQ
A presentation party that girls have when they turn fifteen in Mexico

_____ = 19. EILMGU
Boy Esperanza declared she would marry one day

_____ = 20. ERAIN
Miguel's nickname for Esperanza

JUGGLE 1 ANSWER KEY *Esperanza Rising*

ARVIN	= 1.	VRAIN	
		Setting of the camp where Esperanza and Mama live and work in California	
ABUELITA	= 2.	TELUAIAB	
		Esperanza's maternal grandmother	
AGUASCALIENTES	= 3.	USCELSATEAINAG	
		Location of El Rancho de las Rosas	
MARCO	= 4.	RCMOA	
		Mayor of Aguascalientes	
ORTEGA	= 5.	ERTGAO	
		Esperanza's last name	
CAMPESINOS	= 6.	MCEPISSONA	
		Field-workers	
SIXTO	= 7.	OTXIS	
		Esperanza's father	
RAMONA	= 8.	NAAMOR	
		Esperanza's mother	
PATRONA	= 9.	PANOART	
		Spanish for "head of the household"	
HORTENSIA	= 10.	OHRTEANSI	
		Esperanza's housekeeper	
ALFONSO	= 11.	SAOFLON	
		Hortensia's husband and Miguel's father	
RAILROAD	= 12.	RILAOARD	
		Working there is Miguel's dream job.	
CARMEN	= 13.	ACRNME	
		Gives Mama two hens for her future; the "egg lady"	
MARISOL	= 14.	ILMORAS	
		Esperanza's best friend	
LUIS	= 15.	SLIU	
		Wants to marry Mama	
NUNS	= 16.	SNNU	
		Abuelita's sisters who help Mama and Esperanza get their traveling papers	
PHOENIX	= 17.	PHNIEXO	
		Metaphor Abuelita uses to describe how they will overcome their troubles	
QUINCEANERA	= 18.	AANCREUINEQ	
		A presentation party that girls have when they turn fifteen in Mexico	
MIGUEL	= 19.	EILMGU	
		Boy Esperanza declared she would marry one day	
REINA	= 20.	ERAIN	
		Miguel's nickname for Esperanza	

JUGGLE 2 *Esperanza Rising*

_____ = 1. GTMINIMIRAO
La Migra; sent the strikers to Mexico

_____ = 2. SOSRE
Brought to California by Miguel and Alfonso as a surprise for Mama and Esperanza

_____ = 3. GRTTOO
Contains a statue of Our Lady of Guadalupe

_____ = 4. EWGINSPE
Esperanza's job at the camp when she first arrives

_____ = 5. TRAMA
Wants the workers to band together and strike

_____ = 6. AJNU
Isabel's father

_____ = 7. IFOJSNEA
Isabel's mother

_____ = 8. SACIMAJA
Summer camp parties with music and food held every Saturday night

_____ = 9. NRIAV
Setting of the camp where Esperanza and Mama live and work in California

_____ = 10. SLUPM
Cause the twins to become ill

_____ = 11. IMEANL
Esperanza's new friend who helps watch the twins

_____ = 12. ZZGGAI
Pattern in Abuelita's blanket

_____ = 13. ABELIS
Wants to be the Queen of May

_____ = 14. RETSSKIR
They hide dangerous "surprises" in the harvest.

_____ = 15. OAAKTY
Market owner who is kind to Mexicans

_____ = 16. PTANAI
Bought for Mama but given to the campesino family at the strikers' camp

_____ = 17. VADOACO
Esperanza puts this on her hands to make them soft again

_____ = 18. EESY
Esperanza has to cut these off the potatoes

_____ = 19. TYNNGAHI
What Isabel wants for Christmas

_____ = 20. IRORALDA
Working there is Miguel's dream job.

182

JUGGLE 2 ANSWER KEY *Esperanza Rising*

IMMIGRATION	= 1.	GTMINIMIRAO La Migra; sent the strikers to Mexico
ROSES	= 2.	SOSRE Brought to California by Miguel and Alfonso as a surprise for Mama and Esperanza
GROTTO	= 3.	GRTTOO Contains a statue of Our Lady of Guadalupe
SWEEPING	= 4.	EWGINSPE Esperanza's job at the camp when she first arrives
MARTA	= 5.	TRAMA Wants the workers to band together and strike
JUAN	= 6.	AJNU Isabel's father
JOSEFINA	= 7.	IFOJSNEA Isabel's mother
JAMAICAS	= 8.	SACIMAJA Summer camp parties with music and food held every Saturday night
ARVIN	= 9.	NRIAV Setting of the camp where Esperanza and Mama live and work in California
PLUMS	= 10.	SLUPM Cause the twins to become ill
MELINA	= 11.	IMEANL Esperanza's new friend who helps watch the twins
ZIGZAG	= 12.	ZZGGAI Pattern in Abuelita's blanket
ISABEL	= 13.	ABELIS Wants to be the Queen of May
STRIKERS	= 14.	RETSSKIR They hide dangerous "surprises" in the harvest.
YAKOTA	= 15.	OAAKTY Market owner who is kind to Mexicans
PINATA	= 16.	PTANAI Bought for Mama but given to the campesino family at the strikers' camp
AVOCADO	= 17.	VADOACO Esperanza puts this on her hands to make them soft again
EYES	= 18.	EESY Esperanza has to cut these off the potatoes
ANYTHING	= 19.	TYNNGAHI What Isabel wants for Christmas
RAILROAD	= 20.	IRORALDA Working there is Miguel's dream job.

VOCABULARY RESOURCE MATERIALS

Esperanza Rising Vocabulary

No.	Word	Clue/Definition
1.	ACCOSTING	Approach boldly or aggressively
2.	ACCUSTOMED	Being in the habit of
3.	AMBUSHED	Attacked from a hidden position
4.	ANTICIPATED	Looked forward to; expected
5.	BEREFT	Without or lacking
6.	BESTOWED	Presented as a gift; given
7.	BROODED	Was in a state of gloomy, serious thought
8.	BUOYED	Heartened or inspired; uplifted
9.	CAPRICIOUS	Tending to change abruptly without apparent reason
10.	CAREENING	Wobbling or swerving while in motion, usually at a high speed
11.	CASCADE	Rush down in large amounts
12.	CONDOLENCES	Expressions of sympathy for a person who is suffering sorrow, misfortune, or grief
13.	COPE	Face and deal with responsibilities, problems, or difficulties
14.	CORDIAL	Friendly; warm
15.	CORRUPT	Guilty of dishonest practices; untrustworthy
16.	COT	A light portable bed, esp. one of canvas on a folding frame
17.	DEBRIS	Remains of anything broken down or destroyed; ruins; rubble
18.	DEMEANOR	Conduct; behavior; manner
19.	DEPORTATIONS	Lawful removal of illegal immigrants
20.	DESPONDENT	Depressed; gloomy
21.	DEVOUTLY	Expressing devotion or faith
22.	DOTING	Being excessively fond
23.	DROWSY	Sleepy
24.	DWINDLED	Made smaller or less
25.	ERUPTED	Emerged violently
26.	ESCORTED	Went along with to protect or aid
27.	EXTRAVAGANT	Tending towards extreme or excessive spending
28.	FORLORN	Lonely and sad; unhappy and neglected
29.	FRANTICALLY	Characterized by rapid and disordered or nervous activity
30.	FRAYED	Worn away or tattered along the edges
31.	GINGERLY	With great care or caution
32.	IMMUNIZED	Protected from a disease
33.	INDEBTED	Owing for favors or kindness received
34.	INFURIATED	Very angry
35.	INTENT	Sharply focused on something
36.	JALOPY	Falling apart automobile
37.	LAPEL	Continuation of a collar down the front of a coat or shirt
38.	MAKESHIFT	Something made from whatever materials are available, rather than usual means

No.	Word	Clue/Definition
39.	MARVELED	Looked at with wonder, admiration, or shock
40.	MENACING	Threatening to cause evil, harm, or injury
41.	MESMERIZED	Spellbound; fascinated
42.	MONOTONOUS	Lacking in variety; boring
43.	MUSSED	Messy or untidy; rumpled
44.	OPTIMISM	Characteristic in which someone looks on the more positive side of events or conditions and expects the most positive outcome
45.	PENETRATE	Pierce or pass into or through
46.	PERSISTENT	Determined; refusing to give up
47.	PLAITED	Braided
48.	PREOCCUPIED	Completely lost in thought
49.	PUNGENT	Sour or biting smell or taste
50.	RECLINING	Leaning back
51.	REGAL	Grand; fit for royalty
52.	RELAPSE	Return of a disease or illness after partial recovery from it
53.	RELUCTANTLY	Unwillingly; disinclined
54.	RENEGADES	Outlaws; rebels
55.	RESENTMENT	Feeling of displeasure from a sense of being injured or offended
56.	RESOUNDING	Making an echoing sound
57.	RETRIEVED	Recovered or regained
58.	RIVETED	Fastened (the eye, attention, etc.) firmly to something
59.	SALVAGE	Saving something from fire, danger, etc.
60.	SCORN	Treat or regard with disrespect or shame
61.	SCYTHE	Tool with a long, single-edged blade set at an angle on a long, curved handle, used in cutting long grass, grain, etc. by hand
62.	SERENADED	Entertained with a vocal or instrumental performance of music outdoors at night, esp. by a lover under the window of his sweetheart
63.	SHRINE	Structure or place blessed or devoted to some saint, holy person, or god, as an altar, chapel, church, or temple
64.	SKEINS	Lengths of thread or yarn wound in loose, long coils
65.	SOLEMNLY	Causing serious mood
66.	SPEWING	Shooting out forcefully, usually in an uncontrolled manner
67.	SQUALOR	Condition of filth and misery
68.	STAGNANT	Not flowing or running, as water, air, etc.
69.	STRIKE	Refuse to do work because of an argument or disagreement with an employer over payment or working conditions
70.	SUPPLENESS	Flexibility
71.	SUSCEPTIBLE	Easily influenced; weak
72.	TALLOW	Solid fat taken from animals; used in making candles, soaps, lubricants, etc.
73.	TAUNTING	Teasing

No.	Word	Clue/Definition
74.	TAUT	Tightly drawn; tense
75.	TORMENTED	Experiencing intense pain, especially mental pain
76.	TORRENT	Stream of water flowing with great speed, force, and violence
77.	UNDULATING	Having a wave-like or rippled form or surface
78.	VALISE	Small piece of luggage
79.	VAPORS	Visible breath, as fog, mist, steam, smoke, or gas
80.	VENOM	Poison
81.	WEARY	Tired
82.	WILTED	Limp; drooped; sagging or falling over
83.	YEARNING	Unsatisfied desire

VOCABULARY WORD SEARCH - Esperanza Rising

```
R E T R I E V E D E Z I R E M S E M Z C
J J S I R B E D T M H R P D R R Q W P B
A V C C Y M K P O J Z E D E T B E D N I
L J Y F O Y U E T T D S C D Y Y B G T B
O B T Y D R R G X E I E Q A S P T M A T
P U H V R U T D M B R N C N T O M L F L
Y O E O P W G E G G D T G E R K D I S Y
P Y C T S C A T D E M M J R I N H B Q Q
R E E S C N T I T W U E E E K S R R U T
E D E P O R T A T I O N S S E S I L A V
C R B R R L I L U O T T D K H V S L L V
L S C J N R E P Q N R S A U E R L H O F
I P O T U T C M D C T M A T L O I T R Z
N E T F N V W A N R Y I E L W A U N S G
I W N E P L E I S L O D N N V A T N E M
N I T R C T A N L C Y W Q G T A I I Q H
G N B E O K R Y O T A R S Q Z E G B N Z
I G F B P J Y F P M E D G Y K W D E M G
F R A Y E D E S S U M D E S R O P A V M
```

BEREFT	INTENT	SKEINS
BUOYED	JALOPY	SOLEMNLY
CASCADE	MAKESHIFT	SPEWING
COPE	MESMERIZED	SQUALOR
CORRUPT	MUSSED	STRIKE
COT	PLAITED	TALLOW
DEBRIS	RECLINING	TAUNTING
DEMEANOR	REGAL	TAUT
DEPORTATIONS	RESENTMENT	TORMENTED
DOTING	RETRIEVED	TORRENT
DROWSY	RIVETED	UNDULATING
ERUPTED	SALVAGE	VALISE
ESCORTED	SCORN	VAPORS
FRAYED	SCYTHE	VENOM
INDEBTED	SERENADED	WEARY
INFURIATED	SHRINE	WILTED

VOCABULARY WORD SEARCH ANSWER KEY - Esperanza Rising

BEREFT	INTENT	SKEINS
BUOYED	JALOPY	SOLEMNLY
CASCADE	MAKESHIFT	SPEWING
COPE	MESMERIZED	SQUALOR
CORRUPT	MUSSED	STRIKE
COT	PLAITED	TALLOW
DEBRIS	RECLINING	TAUNTING
DEMEANOR	REGAL	TAUT
DEPORTATIONS	RESENTMENT	TORMENTED
DOTING	RETRIEVED	TORRENT
DROWSY	RIVETED	UNDULATING
ERUPTED	SALVAGE	VALISE
ESCORTED	SCORN	VAPORS
FRAYED	SCYTHE	VENOM
INDEBTED	SERENADED	WEARY
INFURIATED	SHRINE	WILTED

VOCABULARY CROSSWORD - Esperanza Rising

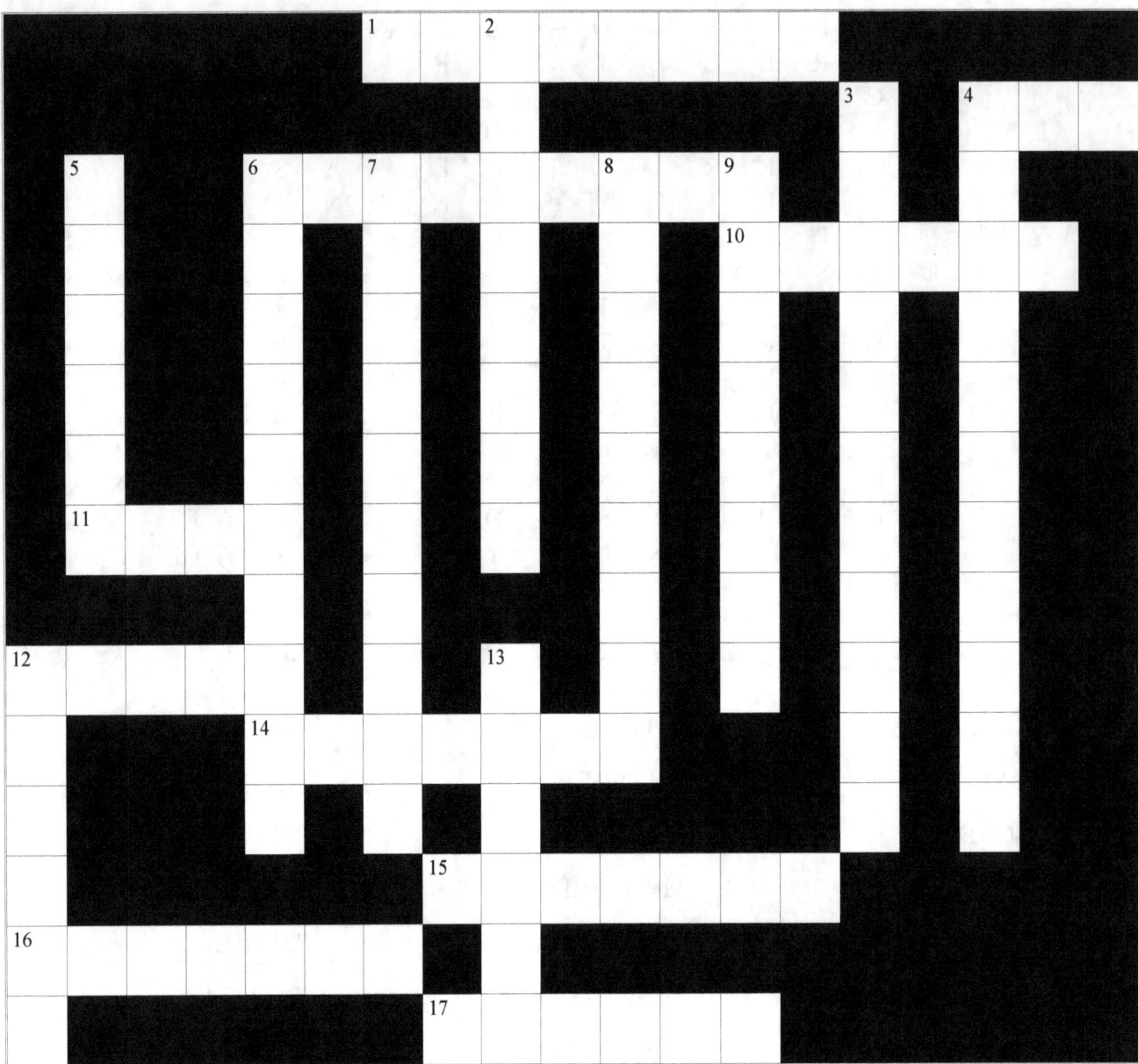

Across
1. Attacked from a hidden position
4. Light, portable bed, esp. one of canvas on a folding frame
6. Approaching boldly or aggressively
10. Sharply focused on something
11. Tightly drawn; tense
12. Poison
14. Emerged violently
15. Fastened (the eye, attention, etc.) firmly to something
16. Saving something from fire, danger, etc.
17. Remains of anything broken down or destroyed; ruins; rubble

Down
2. Presented as a gift; given
3. Looked forward to; expected
4. Expressions of sympathy for a person who is suffering sorrow, misfortune or grief
5. Without; lacking
6. Being in the habit of
7. Tending to change abruptly without apparent reason
8. Protected from a disease
9. With great care or caution
12. Small piece of luggage
13. Refuse to do work because of a disagreement with an employer over pay or conditions

VOCABULARY CROSSWORD ANSWER KEY - Esperanza Rising

			¹A	²B	U	S	H	E	D			
				E						³A	⁴C	O	T
	⁵B	⁶A	C	C	⁷O	S	⁸T	⁹I	N	G		N	O	
	E	C		A		P		O		W		¹⁰I	N	T	E	N	T
	R	C		P		O		M		E		N		I	D
	E	U		R		W		M		E		C		P		O
	F	S		I		E		U		D		I		L
¹¹T	A	U	T		C		D		N			R		P			E
		T			I				I			R		A			N
¹²V	E	N	O	M			O		¹³S		E		Y		T		C
A				¹⁴E	R	U	P	T	E	D				E		E
L				D			S		R					D		S
I					¹⁵R	I	V	E	T	E	D			
¹⁶S	A	L	V	A	G	E		K					
E					¹⁷D	E	B	R	I	S			

Across
1. Attacked from a hidden position
4. Light, portable bed, esp. one of canvas on a folding frame
6. Approaching boldly or aggressively
10. Sharply focused on something
11. Tightly drawn; tense
12. Poison
14. Emerged violently
15. Fastened (the eye, attention, etc.) firmly to something
16. Saving something from fire, danger, etc.
17. Remains of anything broken down or destroyed; ruins; rubble

Down
2. Presented as a gift; given
3. Looked forward to; expected
4. Expressions of sympathy for a person who is suffering sorrow, misfortune or grief
5. Without; lacking
6. Being in the habit of
7. Tending to change abruptly without apparent reason
8. Protected from a disease
9. With great care or caution
12. Small piece of luggage
13. Refuse to do work because of a disagreement with an employer over pay or conditions

VOCABULARY MATCHING 1 *Esperanza Rising*

____ 1. YEARNING A. Falling apart automobile

____ 2. IMMUNIZED B. Protected from a disease

____ 3. FORLORN C. Grand; fit for royalty

____ 4. DWINDLED D. Characteristic in which someone looks on the more positive side of events or conditions and expects the most positive outcome

____ 5. DESPONDENT E. Visible breath, as fog, mist, steam, smoke, or gas

____ 6. COT F. Approach boldly or aggressively

____ 7. CONDOLENCES G. Saving something from fire, danger, etc.

____ 8. CAPRICIOUS H. Depressed; gloomy

____ 9. BEREFT I. A light portable bed, esp. one of canvas on a folding frame

____ 10. JALOPY J. Easily influenced; weak

____ 11. MENACING K. Without or lacking

____ 12. VAPORS L. Threatening to cause evil, harm, or injury

____ 13. SUSCEPTIBLE M. Expressions of sympathy for a person who is suffering sorrow, misfortune, or grief

____ 14. SQUALOR N. Lonely and sad; unhappy and neglected

____ 15. SHRINE O. Tending to change abruptly without apparent reason

____ 16. SALVAGE P. Structure or place blessed or devoted to some saint, holy person, or god, as an altar, chapel, church, or temple

____ 17. RESENTMENT Q. Made smaller or less

____ 18. REGAL R. Feeling of displeasure from a sense of being injured or offended

____ 19. OPTIMISM S. Condition of filth and misery

____ 20. ACCOSTING T. Unsatisfied desire

VOCABULARY MATCHING 1 ANSWER KEY *Esperanza Rising*

T	1.	YEARNING	A.	Falling apart automobile
B	2.	IMMUNIZED	B.	Protected from a disease
N	3.	FORLORN	C.	Grand; fit for royalty
Q	4.	DWINDLED	D.	Characteristic in which someone looks on the more positive side of events or conditions and expects the most positive outcome
H	5.	DESPONDENT	E.	Visible breath, as fog, mist, steam, smoke, or gas
I	6.	COT	F.	Approach boldly or aggressively
M	7.	CONDOLENCES	G.	Saving something from fire, danger, etc.
O	8.	CAPRICIOUS	H.	Depressed; gloomy
K	9.	BEREFT	I.	A light portable bed, esp. one of canvas on a folding frame
A	10.	JALOPY	J.	Easily influenced; weak
L	11.	MENACING	K.	Without or lacking
E	12.	VAPORS	L.	Threatening to cause evil, harm, or injury
J	13.	SUSCEPTIBLE	M.	Expressions of sympathy for a person who is suffering sorrow, misfortune, or grief
S	14.	SQUALOR	N.	Lonely and sad; unhappy and neglected
P	15.	SHRINE	O.	Tending to change abruptly without apparent reason
G	16.	SALVAGE	P.	Structure or place blessed or devoted to some saint, holy person, or god, as an altar, chapel, church, or temple
R	17.	RESENTMENT	Q.	Made smaller or less
C	18.	REGAL	R.	Feeling of displeasure from a sense of being injured or offended
D	19.	OPTIMISM	S.	Condition of filth and misery
F	20.	ACCOSTING	T.	Unsatisfied desire

VOCABULARY MATCHING 2 *Esperanza Rising*

____ 1. VALISE A. Heartened or inspired; uplifted

____ 2. EXTRAVAGANT B. Leaning back

____ 3. DROWSY C. Rush down in large amounts

____ 4. DEPORTATIONS D. Was in a state of gloomy, serious thought

____ 5. COT E. Lawful removal of illegal immigrants

____ 6. CONDOLENCES F. With great care or caution

____ 7. CASCADE G. Tending towards extreme or excessive spending

____ 8. BUOYED H. A light portable bed, esp. one of canvas on a folding frame

____ 9. BROODED I. Looked forward to; expected

____ 10. GINGERLY J. Braided

____ 11. MARVELED K. Messy or untidy; rumpled

____ 12. TAUT L. Flexibility

____ 13. SUPPLENESS M. Tightly drawn; tense

____ 14. SERENADED N. Small piece of luggage

____ 15. RIVETED O. Looked at with wonder, admiration, or shock

____ 16. RENEGADES P. Expressions of sympathy for a person who is suffering sorrow, misfortune, or grief

____ 17. RECLINING Q. Sleepy

____ 18. PLAITED R. Fastened (the eye, attention, etc.) firmly to something

____ 19. MUSSED S. Outlaws; rebels

____ 20. ANTICIPATED T. Entertained with a vocal or instrumental performance of music outdoors at night, esp. by a lover under the window of his sweetheart

VOCABULARY MATCHING 2 ANSWER KEY *Esperanza Rising*

N	1.	VALISE	A.	Heartened or inspired; uplifted
G	2.	EXTRAVAGANT	B.	Leaning back
Q	3.	DROWSY	C.	Rush down in large amounts
E	4.	DEPORTATIONS	D.	Was in a state of gloomy, serious thought
H	5.	COT	E.	Lawful removal of illegal immigrants
P	6.	CONDOLENCES	F.	With great care or caution
C	7.	CASCADE	G.	Tending towards extreme or excessive spending
A	8.	BUOYED	H.	A light portable bed, esp. one of canvas on a folding frame
D	9.	BROODED	I.	Looked forward to; expected
F	10.	GINGERLY	J.	Braided
O	11.	MARVELED	K.	Messy or untidy; rumpled
M	12.	TAUT	L.	Flexibility
L	13.	SUPPLENESS	M.	Tightly drawn; tense
T	14.	SERENADED	N.	Small piece of luggage
R	15.	RIVETED	O.	Looked at with wonder, admiration, or shock
S	16.	RENEGADES	P.	Expressions of sympathy for a person who is suffering sorrow, misfortune, or grief
B	17.	RECLINING	Q.	Sleepy
J	18.	PLAITED	R.	Fastened (the eye, attention, etc.) firmly to something
K	19.	MUSSED	S.	Outlaws; rebels
I	20.	ANTICIPATED	T.	Entertained with a vocal or instrumental performance of music outdoors at night, esp. by a lover under the window of his sweetheart

VOCABULARY JUGGLE LETTERS 1 *Esperanza Rising*

_____ = 1. PLUSEIBSECT
Easily influenced; weak

_____ = 2. OOLRFNR
Lonely and sad; unhappy and neglected

_____ = 3. EDILDWND
Made smaller or less

_____ = 4. EDDTNESNPO
Depressed; gloomy

_____ = 5. NEMDRAOE
Conduct; behavior; manner

_____ = 6. TCO
A light portable bed, esp. one of canvas on a folding frame

_____ = 7. CSNOEDCENLO
Expressions of sympathy for a person who is suffering sorrow, misfortune, or grief

_____ = 8. DEOBYU
Heartened or inspired; uplifted

_____ = 9. ITDPATACINE
Looked forward to; expected

_____ = 10. IMUZIEMDN
Protected from a disease

_____ = 11. ADRTIFUNIE
Very angry

_____ = 12. NEISKS
Lengths of thread or yarn wound in loose, long coils

_____ = 13. LEASGVA
Saving something from fire, danger, etc.

_____ = 14. ETESNRMETN
Feeling of displeasure from a sense of being injured or offended

_____ = 15. ELARG
Grand; fit for royalty

_____ = 16. PETLDIA
Braided

_____ = 17. TMSPIMOI
Characteristic in which someone looks on the more positive side of events or conditions and expects the most positive outcome

_____ = 18. CAENNMIG
Threatening to cause evil, harm, or injury

_____ = 19. YPLOAJ
Falling apart automobile

_____ = 20. AIOSTNCGC
Approach boldly or aggressively

VOCABULARY JUGGLE LETTERS 1 ANSWER KEY *Esperanza Rising*

SUSCEPTIBLE	= 1.	PLUSEIBSECT Easily influenced; weak
FORLORN	= 2.	OOLRFNR Lonely and sad; unhappy and neglected
DWINDLED	= 3.	EDILDWND Made smaller or less
DESPONDENT	= 4.	EDDTNESNPO Depressed; gloomy
DEMEANOR	= 5.	NEMDRAOE Conduct; behavior; manner
COT	= 6.	TCO A light portable bed, esp. one of canvas on a folding frame
CONDOLENCES	= 7.	CSNOEDCENLO Expressions of sympathy for a person who is suffering sorrow, misfortune, or grief
BUOYED	= 8.	DEOBYU Heartened or inspired; uplifted
ANTICIPATED	= 9.	ITDPATACINE Looked forward to; expected
IMMUNIZED	= 10.	IMUZIEMDN Protected from a disease
INFURIATED	= 11.	ADRTIFUNIE Very angry
SKEINS	= 12.	NEISKS Lengths of thread or yarn wound in loose, long coils
SALVAGE	= 13.	LEASGVA Saving something from fire, danger, etc.
RESENTMENT	= 14.	ETESNRMETN Feeling of displeasure from a sense of being injured or offended
REGAL	= 15.	ELARG Grand; fit for royalty
PLAITED	= 16.	PETLDIA Braided
OPTIMISM	= 17.	TMSPIMOI Characteristic in which someone looks on the more positive side of events or conditions and expects the most positive outcome
MENACING	= 18.	CAENNMIG Threatening to cause evil, harm, or injury
JALOPY	= 19.	YPLOAJ Falling apart automobile
ACCOSTING	= 20.	AIOSTNCGC Approach boldly or aggressively

VOCABULARY JUGGLE LETTERS 2 *Esperanza Rising*

_____ = 1. NNRAEGYI
Unsatisfied desire

_____ = 2. DDIBTENE
Owing for favors or kindness received

_____ = 3. RNIALLYFACT
Characterized by rapid and disordered or nervous activity

_____ = 4. TTAGVEAXNRA
Tending towards extreme or excessive spending

_____ = 5. RUEPEDT
Emerged violently

_____ = 6. UETLDVOY
Expressing devotion or faith

_____ = 7. DRBESI
Remains of anything broken down or destroyed; ruins; rubble

_____ = 8. EDOEONCLCNS
Expressions of sympathy for a person who is suffering sorrow, misfortune, or grief

_____ = 9. SIAIRPUOCC
Tending to change abruptly without apparent reason

_____ = 10. ELALP
Continuation of a collar down the front of a coat or shirt

_____ = 11. GNENPUT
Sour or biting smell or taste

_____ = 12. OAVSRP
Visible breath, as fog, mist, steam, smoke, or gas

_____ = 13. NNIALTUUGD
Having a wave-like or rippled form or surface

_____ = 14. TRMEOENTD
Experiencing intense pain, especially mental pain

_____ = 15. ISPTLBUCESE
Easily influenced; weak

_____ = 16. SNTNTGAA
Not flowing or running, as water, air, etc.

_____ = 17. QLARUOS
Condition of filth and misery

_____ = 18. HERINS
Structure or place blessed or devoted to some saint, holy person, or god, as an altar, chapel, church, or temple

_____ = 19. RGAEDESNE
Outlaws; rebels

_____ = 20. TBEEFR
Without or lacking

VOCABULARY JUGGLE LETTERS 2 ANSWER KEY *Esperanza Rising*

YEARNING	= 1.	NNRAEGYI Unsatisfied desire
INDEBTED	= 2.	DDIBTENE Owing for favors or kindness received
FRANTICALLY	= 3.	RNIALLYFACT Characterized by rapid and disordered or nervous activity
EXTRAVAGANT	= 4.	TTAGVEAXNRA Tending towards extreme or excessive spending
ERUPTED	= 5.	RUEPEDT Emerged violently
DEVOUTLY	= 6.	UETLDVOY Expressing devotion or faith
DEBRIS	= 7.	DRBESI Remains of anything broken down or destroyed; ruins; rubble
CONDOLENCES	= 8.	EDOEONCLCNS Expressions of sympathy for a person who is suffering sorrow, misfortune, or grief
CAPRICIOUS	= 9.	SIAIRPUOCC Tending to change abruptly without apparent reason
LAPEL	= 10.	ELALP Continuation of a collar down the front of a coat or shirt
PUNGENT	= 11.	GNENPUT Sour or biting smell or taste
VAPORS	= 12.	OAVSRP Visible breath, as fog, mist, steam, smoke, or gas
UNDULATING	= 13.	NNIALTUUGD Having a wave-like or rippled form or surface
TORMENTED	= 14.	TRMEOENTD Experiencing intense pain, especially mental pain
SUSCEPTIBLE	= 15.	ISPTLBUCESE Easily influenced; weak
STAGNANT	= 16.	SNTNTGAA Not flowing or running, as water, air, etc.
SQUALOR	= 17.	QLARUOS Condition of filth and misery
SHRINE	= 18.	HERINS Structure or place blessed or devoted to some saint, holy person, or god, as an altar, chapel, church, or temple
RENEGADES	= 19.	RGAEDESNE Outlaws; rebels
BEREFT	= 20.	TBEEFR Without or lacking

www.ingramcontent.com/pod-product-compliance
Lightning Source LLC
Chambersburg PA
CBHW051405070526
44584CB00023B/3299